Demystifying
ROBOTICS

S VELMURUGAN

B SATHEESH KUMAR

P YUVARAJA

Dedicated to Our Families

About the Authors

Dr. S. Velmurugan is a dynamic academician and researcher in the field of Computer Science, with a career spanning both industry and academia. An alumnus of Annamalai University, he holds a Ph.D. in Computer Science with a specialization in forensic image analysis. His doctoral research introduced a novel computer vision-based forgery detection system, pushing the boundaries of digital image processing in the realm of forensic science. Currently serving as an Assistant Professor in the Department of Computer Science with Data Analytics at Kongunadu Arts and Science College (Autonomous), Coimbatore, Tamil Nadu, Dr. Velmurugan combines his industry expertise—gained during his tenure as a Storage Administrator at Right Tech Solutions Ltd., Chennai—with his passion for teaching and research. He has contributed to several prestigious research initiatives, including his role as a Project Fellow under the Government of India's DST-PURSE (Phase II) program, where he advanced innovative approaches to computational challenges. His scholarly work includes 15 research articles published in leading international journals such as Elsevier and IEEE, as well as presentations at numerous national and international conferences. As a respected reviewer and editorial board member, Dr. Velmurugan is affiliated with prominent platforms like the American Journal of Artificial Intelligence (USA), the International Journal of Computing and Digital Systems (University of Bahrain), and The Nucleus (UGC Care Listed Journal, 2024). His expertise has also been sought by international forums, including the African Federation of Operational Research Societies (AFROS) and the International Conference on Decision Aid Sciences and Applications (DASA). Dr. Velmurugan has authored one book and continues to make significant contributions to the fields of image processing, computer vision, and pattern recognition. His work embodies a commitment to advancing knowledge and nurturing the next generation of computing professionals.

Dr. Satheesh Kumar B is presently serving as an Assistant Professor in the School of Computing Science and Engineering, Galgotias University, Greater Noida, India. He completed his doctorate on the topic of Image Processing from Annamalai Unviresity, Chidambaram. His doctoral dissertation outlines various research directions and opens up future avenues in Video Retrieval. He has more than 18 publications and 5 book chapter in National and international conferences, peer-reviewed International Journal proceedings indexed in Scopus, SCIE, and SCI databases, and 2 Patent. He has more than 10 years of teaching experience and 1 years of Industry experience. His research area of interest is Image Processing, Video Retrieval, Big Data Analytics, Computer Vision and Deep Learning.

Mr. P. Yuvaraja is a vibrant academician with over 19 years of distinguished experience in teaching and research. He is currently pursuing his Ph.D. at Periyar University and serves as an Assistant Professor and Programmer in the Department of Computer and Information Science at Annamalai University. He earned his M.Sc. in Applied Science (Computer Technology) from Mahendra Engineering College, Mallasamudram, and his M.Phil. in Computer Science from the prestigious Annamalai University, reflecting a strong academic foundation and expertise in his field. Mr. Yuvaraja has an impressive scholarly record, with 8 research articles published in reputed journals and 9 papers presented at various national and international conferences. His work highlights a dedication to advancing knowledge and fostering innovation in computer science and information technology. With his dynamic approach to mentoring and education, he continues to inspire students and contribute significantly to academia through his expertise, commitment, and passion for lifelong learning.

Contents   Page No

About the Book

"Robot Demystifying" Unlocking the Foundations and Future of Robotics offers a uniquely accessible journey into the world of robotics, bridging the gap between complex robotic technologies and everyday understanding. This book stands out by providing a holistic approach that unites robotics theory, hands-on applications, and the latest trends, making it an invaluable guide for readers of all backgrounds—whether they are newcomers, students, or seasoned engineers.

The book begins with the origins of robotics and the evolution of robotic generations, tracing how these machines transitioned from rudimentary automated tools to sophisticated systems used in diverse fields today. Through detailed explanations of robot anatomy, classifications, and configurations, readers gain insight into the mechanics that drive robotic movement and manipulation.

A distinguishing aspect of **"Robot Demystifying"** is its focus on the cutting-edge technologies that empower robots, such as advanced sensors, machine vision systems, and artificial intelligence-driven decision-making. By breaking down the inner workings of sensors, readers learn how robots perceive their environment, and through machine vision systems, how they interpret and act on visual data. The book also explores innovative gripper designs and introduces readers to robotic kinematics and path planning, explaining how these concepts enable precise, complex robotic motions.

Further adding to its uniqueness, **"Robot Demystifying"** devotes an entire section to programming languages in robotics, detailing how languages like Python, C++, and ROS (Robot Operating System) bring robots to life and how programming is pivotal in adapting robotics to specialized tasks and environments. This section also highlights the recent shifts in programming for robotics, examining how new languages and frameworks are redefining the field.

With its forward-looking perspective on trends, challenges, and ethical considerations in robotics, "Robot Demystifying" is not just a guide but a complete reference. It equips readers to not only understand robotics today but also to anticipate and contribute to the innovations of tomorrow.

Preface

Robotics has long been a field associated with high-tech marvels and futuristic concepts. Yet, the reality is that robots are no longer confined to science fiction. They have become an integral part of industries ranging from manufacturing and healthcare to agriculture and entertainment. With rapid advancements in technology, robotics is poised to revolutionize the way we live and work. However, despite its growing influence, the complexities of robotics can often appear daunting.

This book, **"Robot Demystifying"** aims to simplify and clarify the world of robotics, making it accessible to anyone with an interest in understanding this exciting field. Whether you are a student, engineer, researcher, or just a curious enthusiast, this book provides a comprehensive and easy-to-understand guide to the key concepts, technologies, and applications of robotics.

In the following chapters, we take you on a journey that starts with the basics—defining what a robot is, tracing the history of robotics, and exploring the anatomy and classifications of robotic systems. From there, we dive into the crucial technologies that power modern robots, such as sensors, machine vision, and artificial intelligence. You will learn how robots interact with their environment, how they "see" and "feel," and how they manipulate objects with incredible precision.

One of the unique aspects of this book is its emphasis on programming. We explore the role of various programming languages in robotics, offering insights into the tools that allow engineers to bring robots to life. With a focus on recent trends in programming, we examine how the evolution of software continues to shape the capabilities of robots.

Throughout the book, we emphasize practical applications, from industrial robots performing complex assembly tasks to robots navigating in unpredictable environments. You will also gain insights into the future of robotics—how emerging technologies, such as autonomous robots and machine learning, are pushing the boundaries of what robots can do.

At its core, "Robot Demystifying" is designed to make the world of robotics understandable and approachable. It is not just a technical manual but a guide to the possibilities and potential of robotics as a transformative force in our society. Whether you are new to robotics or seeking to deepen your knowledge, this book will help you navigate the ever-evolving landscape of robotic technologies.

I hope this book sparks your curiosity and inspires you to explore the fascinating world of robotics. The future of robots is just beginning, and it is my belief that this book will serve as a stepping stone for anyone looking to better understand the forces that are shaping our technological future.

— [Authors]

How This Book Is Organized

This book, Robot Demystifying: Unlocking the Foundations and Future of Robotics, is structured into five comprehensive sections, each designed to provide a clear understanding of robotics from fundamentals to advanced concepts:

Chapter 1: Introduction to Robotics

This chapter lays the foundation by defining what robots are, tracing their history, and exploring their evolution through generations. It delves into robot anatomy, classifications, and the configurations of robotic arms. The chapter concludes by highlighting the growing need for automation in today's world.

Chapter 2: Sensors and Vision Systems in Robotics

Sensors are the sensory organs of robots. This chapter introduces various types of sensors, their applications, and the critical role of machine vision in robotics. It explains the workflow and components of machine vision systems, discusses emerging trends, and explores future advancements in sensors and vision technologies.

Chapter 3: Grippers and Robot Dynamics

Grippers form an essential part of robotic manipulators. This chapter covers the design considerations for grippers, types of gripper mechanisms (mechanical, vacuum, magnetic, soft grippers, etc.), and their applications. It also introduces robotic manipulators, kinematics, and robot dynamics, providing insight into how robots move and interact with their environment.

Chapter 4: Kinematics and Path Planning

This chapter focuses on robot kinematics, both serial and parallel manipulators, and their structural advantages. It explores matrix representations, vector analysis, and path planning techniques, offering a deep dive into the mathematical frameworks that govern robotic motion.

Chapter 5: Programming Languages and Applications

Programming breathes life into robotics. This chapter discusses the role of programming languages in robotics, recent trends, and their applications. It concludes with insights into future directions in robotics programming and how software continues to drive innovation in this field.

Each chapter is crafted to provide readers with a blend of theoretical knowledge and practical applications, equipping them to understand and contribute to the rapidly evolving field of robotics.

Chapter 1

Introduction to Robotics

Robotics is a branch of technology that deals with the design, construction, operation, and application of robots. Robots are automated machines that can perform tasks traditionally carried out by humans. This field integrates various disciplines, including mechanical engineering, electrical engineering, computer science, and artificial intelligence.

1.1 What is a Robot?

A robot is an electro-mechanical device programmed to carry out tasks autonomously or semi-autonomously. Modern robots can range from industrial arms used in manufacturing to humanoid robots designed for social interactions.

Key Components of a Robot

1. **Actuators**: The "muscles" of a robot, allowing it to move or manipulate objects.
2. **Sensors**: Devices that provide feedback to the robot about its environment, enabling perception and adaptation.

3. **Controller**: The brain of the robot, often a computer system or microcontroller that processes data and issues commands to the actuators.
4. **Power Supply**: The source of energy (battery, solar power, or electric grid) that enables the robot to operate.
5. **End-Effector**: The tool or "hand" of a robot, which interacts with the environment, such as a gripper or welding torch.

Basic Types of Robots

1. **Industrial Robots**: Used in manufacturing for repetitive tasks like welding, painting, or assembly.
2. **Humanoid Robots**: Designed to mimic human actions, used in research, entertainment, or customer service.
3. **Mobile Robots**: Autonomous robots that move through environments, including rovers used in space exploration and drones.

Robotics and Automation

Automation is the use of control systems for operating equipment with minimal human intervention. Robotics is a subset of automation, but it goes beyond pre-programmed operations, integrating machine learning and AI to perform more complex, dynamic tasks.

1.2 History of Robot (Origin):

Early Concepts

- **Ancient History**: Early ideas of automatons can be traced to ancient myths, like the Greek legend of Talos (a bronze giant) and the mechanical birds and statues of ancient China and Egypt.
- **1495**: Leonardo da Vinci designed a humanoid robot known as Leonardo's robot. It could sit, wave its arms, and move its head.

20[th]Century

- **1921**: The word "robot" was first introduced by Czech writer Karel Čapek in his play R.U.R. (Rossum's Universal Robots), where robots were depicted as artificial laborers.
- **1942**: Isaac Asimov formulated the "Three Laws of Robotics" in his short story Runaround, establishing ethical guidelines for robots.
- **1956**: George Devol and Joseph Engelberger developed the first commercial robot company,

Unimation, marking the beginning of industrial robotics.

Key Milestones in Robot Development

- **1961**: General Motors installed the first industrial robot, Unimate, in a New Jersey plant for automated tasks like die casting.
- **1968**: The first mobile robot with vision capacity, Shakev, was developed at Stanford Research Institute (SRI).
- **1970**: The Stanford Arm, one of the first computer-controlled robotic arms, was developed.
- **1973**: Cincinnati Milacron's (T3) industrial robot was created, the first mini-computer-controlled electrically actuated robot.
- **1976**: Viking II landed on Mars with a robotic arm that collected soil for analysis.
- **1978**: Unimation Inc. developed the PUMA (Programmable Universal Machine for Assembly) robot, which is still used in education and research labs today.
- **1981**: The first comprehensive textbook on robotics, Robot Manipulators by R. Paul, was published.

- **1982**: Microbot and Rhino developed the first educational robots.
- **1983**: Adept Technology, known for SCARA (Selective Compliance Assembly Robot Arm) robots, was founded.

Robotics in Medicine and Space

- **1995**: Intuitive Surgical formed, paving the way for the design and marketing of surgical robots like the da Vinci Surgical System.
- **1997**: NASA's Sojourner robot rover sent images of Mars back to Earth; Honda unveiled the P3 humanoid robot, leading to the later development of Asimo.
- **2000**: Honda demonstrated Asimo, a humanoid robot capable of walking and interacting with humans.
- **2001**: Sony released the second generation of the Aibo robotic dog, featuring more advanced interactive features.
- **2004**: NASA's Spirit and Opportunity robots explored the surface of Mars and discovered evidence of past water on the planet.

Advanced Robotics and Emerging Trends

- **2007**: Aiko, a humanoid robot capable of "feeling" pain, was created, showcasing early sensory robotics.

- **2009**: The rise of micro-robots and nano-robots marked the integration of biology and engineering, particularly in medical applications.

- **2011**: IBM's Watson defeated human contestants on the game show Jeopardy! using advanced AI, highlighting the capabilities of artificial intelligence in robotics.

- **2013**: Google acquired multiple robotics companies, including Boston Dynamics, pushing research in legged robots and autonomous systems.

- **2015**: SoftBank Robotics released Pepper, a humanoid robot designed to read emotions and interact socially, used in customer service.

- **2016**: Hanson Robotics introduced Sophia, a lifelike humanoid robot, known for its advanced conversational abilities and AI integration.

- **2020**: Boston Dynamics released Spot, a quadruped robot, for commercial use, showcasing its utility in dangerous and industrial environments.

- **2021**: Tesla announced its plans for a humanoid robot, Tesla Bot, aimed at performing repetitive tasks.
- **2022**: Ameca, a humanoid robot with ultra-realistic facial expressions and interaction capabilities, gained attention for its sophisticated AI-driven conversational skills.
- **2023-Present**: Continued developments in AI and robotics are focusing on autonomous systems, humanoid robots for service roles, and advancements in robotics for healthcare, space exploration, and industrial automation.

Key Themes in Modern Robotics

- **AI Integration**: Robots are increasingly integrated with artificial intelligence (AI) and machine learning for improved autonomy and decision-making capabilities.
- **Humanoid Robots**: Humanoid robots like Asimo, Pepper, and Sophia are being designed to interact with humans more naturally in social settings.
- **Autonomous Systems**: Self-driving cars, drones, and delivery robots exemplify the rise of autonomous systems in transportation and logistics.

- **Healthcare Robotics**: Robots like the da Vinci Surgical System revolutionized surgery, and robotics continues to advance in rehabilitation and elderly care.

Robotics has evolved from simple industrial machines to complex autonomous systems, capable of interacting with humans, exploring other planets, and integrating AI for decision-making. The field continues to grow, with new applications in healthcare, social services, and space exploration.

An advance in robotics has closely followed the explosive development of computers and electronics. Initial robot usage was primarily in industrial application such as part/material handling, welding and painting and few in handling of hazardous material. Most initial robots operated in teach-playback mode, and replaced _repetitive'and _back - breaking' tasks. Growth and usage of robots slowed significantly in late 1980's and early 1990's due to —lack of intelligence‖ and —ability to adapt‖ to changing environment – Robots were essentially blind, deaf and dumb!. Last 15 yearsorso, sophisticated sensors and programming allow robots to act much more intelligently, autonomously and react to changes in environments faster.

Present-dayrobots:

1. Used incluttered work spaces in homes and factories,

2. Interact safely with humans in close proximity,

3. Operate autonomously in hazardous environments,

4. Used in entertainment and in improving quality of life.

1.3 Generations of Robot

The development of robots can be categorized into several generations based on their capabilities, technology used, and application domains. Each generation signifies advancements in robot autonomy, control systems, and functionalities, ultimately leading to more intelligent and versatile machines.The various generations of robots areas follows.

First Generation (1950s–1970s): Pre-Programmed Robots

Key Characteristics:

- **Fixed Automation**: Robots in this generation were simple, pre-programmed machines designed for repetitive tasks.

- **Limited Sensing**: They had no or minimal sensing capabilities, relying purely on pre-defined sequences of operations.
- **Manual Programming**: Tasks had to be manually programmed using punch cards or fixed control logic.

Applications:

- Primarily used in **industrial automation**, especially in car manufacturing and assembly lines.

Key Examples:

- **Unimate** (1961): The first industrial robot, designed for assembly line tasks in General Motors factories.
- **Stanford Arm** (1970): One of the earliest computer-controlled robotic arms, developed for research and industrial applications.

Second Generation (1970s–1990s): Programmable Robots with Sensors

Key Characteristics:

- **Programmable**: These robots could be programmed for multiple tasks, enhancing their flexibility.
- **Sensor Integration**: Basic sensors were incorporated, allowing the robots to respond to changes in the environment (e.g., proximity sensors, touch sensors).
- **Feedback Control**: The introduction of feedback loops, enabling real-time monitoring and error correction in robot operations.

Applications:

- **Assembly tasks**, **welding**, and **painting** in the automotive and manufacturing industries.

Key Examples:

- **Cincinnati Milacron's T3 Robot** (1973): One of the earliest mini-computer-controlled robots.
- **PUMA (Programmable Universal Machine for Assembly)** (1978): A versatile robot used in research labs and industrial applications.

Third Generation (1990s–2000s): Autonomous and Adaptive Robots

Key Characteristics:

- **Autonomous Decision Making**: Robots in this generation began to exhibit higher levels of autonomy and could make decisions based on real-time data.

- **AI and Machine Learning Integration**: Basic AI algorithms were introduced, allowing robots to learn from experiences and adapt their behavior.

- **Advanced Sensing**: Enhanced sensor technologies (e.g., cameras, infrared sensors, LIDAR) allowed robots to interact more intelligently with their environments.

Applications:

- **Autonomous systems** in manufacturing, space exploration, medical applications, and home assistance.

Key Examples:

- **Sojourner** (1997): NASA's Mars rover that could navigate the Martian surface and send back images and data to Earth.
- **Honda's ASIMO** (2000): A humanoid robot capable of walking, running, and recognizing faces, marking a significant leap in humanoid robotics.

Fourth Generation (2000s–2010s): Collaborative and Service Robots

Key Characteristics:

- **Collaborative Robots (Cobots)**: Robots designed to work alongside humans in shared workspaces, without the need for safety barriers.
- **Advanced AI and Machine Learning**: Machine learning techniques allowed robots to improve performance and carry out more complex tasks without human intervention.
- **Human-Robot Interaction (HRI)**: Development of robots capable of interacting naturally with humans through speech recognition, gesture control, and emotional response.

Applications:

- **Medical robots, service robots,** and **personal assistants,** with applications ranging from surgery to customer service.

Key Examples:

- **Intuitive Surgical'sDa Vinci System** (1999): A robot-assisted surgical system allowing for precise minimally invasive surgeries.
- **SoftBank Robotics' Pepper** (2015): A social robot capable of recognizing emotions and interacting with customers in retail and service environments.

Fifth Generation (2010s–Present): Intelligent and Autonomous Systems

Key Characteristics:

- **Full Autonomy:** Fifth-generation robots possess high levels of autonomy, with the ability to perform tasks without human intervention or detailed programming.
- **Advanced AI and Cognitive Computing:** Robots are equipped with powerful AI systems that enable

natural language processing, real-time decision-making, and interaction with humans and other robots.

- **Machine Learning and Deep Learning**: These robots continuously improve through machine learning, using massive datasets to enhance their decision-making abilities.

- **Swarm Robotics**: Collaboration between multiple robots working together to accomplish tasks, often used in fields like search-and-rescue and agricultural robotics.

Applications:

- Autonomous vehicles, robotic companions, exploration robots, surgical systems, warehousing robots, and military applications.

Key Examples:

- **Boston Dynamics' Spot** (2020): A quadrupedal robot used in industrial inspections, exploration, and research.

- **Tesla Bot** (2021): A humanoid robot developed to perform repetitive tasks autonomously.

- **Sophia by Hanson Robotics** (2016): A humanoid robot with advanced conversational abilities and realistic facial expressions.

Emerging Trends and Future Generations

Sixth Generation and Beyond:

- **Nano-Robotics**: Tiny robots capable of performing tasks at the cellular level, with potential applications in medicine, such as targeting cancer cells.
- **Biohybrid Robots**: The integration of living tissues with robotic systems, allowing for more lifelike movement and responses.
- **Quantum Computing in Robotics**: The application of quantum algorithms to enhance robot decision-making and processing speed.

Predicted Applications:

- **AI-driven autonomous robots** for space exploration, extreme environment operations, and social companionship in smart homes.
- **Medical nano-robots** that can deliver drugs to specific cells, repair tissues, and perform micro-surgeries.

1.4 Definitionfor Robot

The Robot Institute of America (1969) defines robot as a re-programmable, multi-functional manipulator designed to move materials, parts, tools or specialized devices through various programmed motions for the performance of a variety of tasks.

<u>Asimov's laws of robotics:</u>

1. A robot may not injure a human being or, through in action, allow a human being to come to harm.
2. A robot must obey the orders given it by human beings except where such orders would conflict with the First Law.
3. A robot must protect it sown existence as long as such protection does not conflict with the First or Second Laws.

Robotics system components:

- **Mechanical platforms or hardware base** is a mechanical device, such as a wheeled platform, arm, fixed frame or other construction, capable of interacting with its environment and any other mechanism involve with his capabilities and uses.

- **Sensors** systems is a special feature that rest on or around the robot. This device would be able to provide judgment to the controller with relevant information about the environment and give useful feedback to the robot.

- **Joints** provide more versatility to the robot itself and are not just a point that connects two links or parts that can flex, rotate, revolve and translate. Joints play a very crucial role in the ability of the robot to move in different directions providing more degree of freedom.

- **Controller** functions as the "brain" of the robot. Robots today have controllers that are run by programs - sets of instructions written in code. In other words, it is a computer used to commandthe robot memory and logic. So it, be able to work independently and automatically.

- **Power Source** is the main source of energy to fulfill all the robots needs. It could be a source of direct current as a battery, or alternate current from a power plant, solar energy, hydraulics or gas.

- **Artificial intelligence** represents the ability of computers to "think" in ways similar to human beings. Present day "AI" does allow machines to mimic certain simple human thought processes, but cannot begin to match the quickness and complexity of the brain. On the other hand, not all robots possess this type of capability. It requires a lot of programming and sophisticates controllers and sensorial ability of the robot to reach this level.

- **Actuators** are the muscles of robot. An actuator is a mechanism for activating process control equipment by the use of pneumatic, hydraulic or electronic signals. There are several types of actuators in robotic arms namely synchronous actuator – brush and brushless DC servo, stepper motor and asynchronous actuator – AC servo motor, traction motor, pneumatic, hydraulic.

1.5 Classification of Robot

Robots can be classified based on various criteria, such as their level of autonomy, application domains, control methods, structure, and locomotion. Below is a detailed classification based on some common factors. The ways of classifying a robot as follows

1.5.1. Based on Level of Autonomy

a) Manual Robots:

- Operated entirely by humans, often via remote control or direct mechanical manipulation.
- Example: **Bomb disposal robots**, operated remotely by humans to handle dangerous tasks.

b) Automated Robots:

- Pre-programmed to perform repetitive tasks without human intervention.
- Follow strict instructions and lack flexibility in changing environments.
- Example: **Assembly line robots** used in the automotive industry.

c) Semi-Autonomous Robots:

- Can perform tasks with some level of autonomy but may require human intervention in certain situations.
- Example: **Autonomous drones** for delivery services, which may need human control in complex airspaces.

d) Fully Autonomous Robots:

- Capable of performing tasks and making decisions independently, with no human involvement.
- Equipped with advanced AI and sensors for real-time decision-making.
- Example: **Self-driving cars** and **robotic vacuum cleaners** (e.g., Roomba).

1.5.2. Based on Application

a) Industrial Robots:

- Used in manufacturing processes like assembly, welding, painting, and packaging.
- Designed for repetitive tasks in highly controlled environments.
- Example: **Fanuc robots** in car manufacturing plants.

b) Service Robots:

- Designed to assist humans in everyday tasks in domestic or commercial settings.
- Example: **Pepper** by SoftBank Robotics, a humanoid robot for customer service and retail.

c) Medical Robots:

- Utilized in medical procedures, surgeries, or patient care.
- Example: **Da Vinci Surgical System** for minimally invasive surgeries.

d) Military Robots:

- Used for defense and military operations such as reconnaissance, surveillance, and combat.
- Example: **Boston Dynamics' BigDog**, a quadruped robot designed for military applications.

e) Space Robots:

- Designed for space exploration and performing tasks in extraterrestrial environments.
- Example: **NASA's Mars Rover** (Spirit, Opportunity) for exploring the Martian surface.

f) Entertainment Robots:

- Created for amusement, toys, and personal entertainment.
- Example: **Sony's Aibo**, a robotic dog used as an interactive companion.

g) Agricultural Robots:

- Employed in agriculture for planting, harvesting, and monitoring crops.
- Example: **Harvest CROO Robotics**, designed to pick strawberries in large-scale farming.

1.5.3. Based on Control Method

a) Teleoperated Robots:

- Controlled remotely by a human operator using a control device.
- Typically used in dangerous or hard-to-reach environments.
- Example: **Teleoperated drones** used in search-and-rescue missions.

b) Autonomous Robots:

- Perform tasks on their own, with decision-making capabilities based on sensor input and AI algorithms.
- Example: **Autonomous warehouse robots** that organize and transport goods.

c) Hybrid Robots:

- Can switch between autonomous operation and manual control depending on the situation.
- Example: **UAVs (Unmanned Aerial Vehicles)**, which can be both autonomous and remotely piloted.

1.5.4. Based on Mobility

a) Stationary Robots:

- Robots that remain fixed in one location and perform tasks within their working space.
- Common in industrial settings, where they are bolted to a platform or workbench.
- Example: **SCARA robots** (Selective Compliance Articulated Robot Arm) used in assembly operations.

b) Mobile Robots:

- Capable of moving from one location to another, often equipped with wheels, tracks, or legs for navigation.
- Example: **Autonomous Mobile Robots (AMRs)** used in warehouses for inventory management.

1.5.5. Based on Structure

a) Articulated Robots:

- Robots with rotary joints that allow flexible movement, often used in industrial applications.
- Typically have a base and multiple arm segments.
- Example: **PUMA robot** used in manufacturing and research.

b) SCARA Robots:

- Selective Compliance Articulated Robot Arms, used for precision tasks like assembly.
- Have a fixed base and are designed for operations that require a high degree of accuracy.
- Example: **Adept SCARA robots** used for assembly tasks.

c) Delta Robots:

- Parallel robots with three arms connected to a common base, used for fast, precise pick-and-place tasks.
- Example: **ABB's FlexPicker** used in packaging and sorting.

d) Cartesian Robots:

- Operate on three linear axes (X, Y, Z), allowing for straightforward movements.
- Commonly used for tasks that involves precise and repetitive actions.
- Example: **3D printers** and **CNC machines**.

e) Cylindrical Robots:

- Operate within a cylindrical-shaped work envelope, combining linear and rotary movements.
- Example: **Kawasaki cylindrical robots** used in assembly and packaging.

f) Spherical Robots:

- Feature a spherical work envelope with rotating joints, used in applications that require large, sweeping motions.
- Example: **Spherical coordinate robots** for welding and material handling.

g) Humanoid Robots:

- Robots designed to resemble the human form, with arms, legs, and a head, often used for research, service, or interaction purposes.
- Example: **Honda's ASIMO**, a humanoid robot capable of walking, running, and climbing stairs.

1.5.6. Based on Locomotion

a) Wheeled Robots:

- Use wheels for movement, suitable for flat surfaces.
- Example: **Autonomous delivery robots** used in logistics and retail.

b) Legged Robots:

- Use legs to walk or climb, suitable for rough terrain or human-like mobility.
- Example: **Boston Dynamics' Spot**, a quadruped robot for inspection and exploration.

c) Tracked Robots:

- Equipped with tracks for navigating uneven terrains, similar to tanks.
- Example: **Tracked robots** used in military and bomb disposal operations.

d) Flying Robots (Drones):

- Aerial robots capable of flight, typically used for surveillance, delivery, or exploration.
- Example: **DJI's Phantom drones** used in aerial photography and mapping.

e) Swimming Robots:

- Robots designed for underwater exploration and tasks.
- Example: **Autonomous underwater vehicles (AUVs)** used for deep-sea exploration.

1.5.7. Based on the Degrees of Freedom (DOF)

a) Low DOF Robots:

- Robots with limited movement capabilities, typically one to three degrees of freedom.
- Example: Simple pick-and-place arms in factories.

b) High DOF Robots:

- Robots with more complex motion capabilities, often 6 or more degrees of freedom, allowing for a wide range of tasks.

- Example: **6-axis industrial robotic arms** used in welding, painting, and assembly.

1.6 Robot Anatomy

Robot anatomy refers to the structural components and subsystems that make up a robot. Understanding the anatomy of a robot is essential to grasp how these machines perform tasks, interact with their environment, and process information.

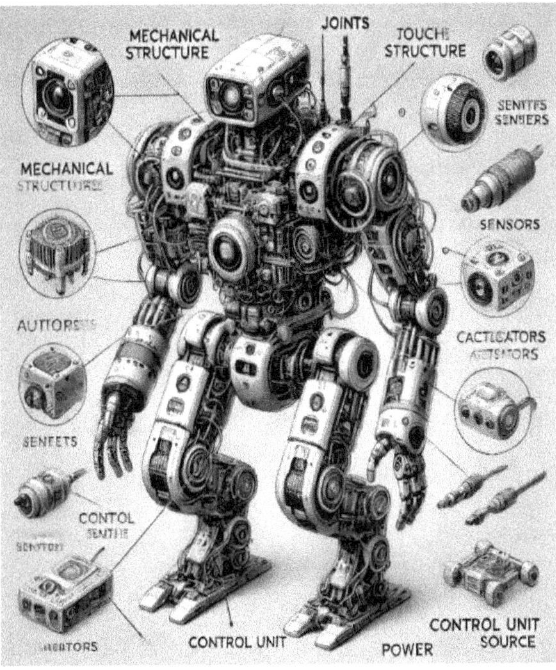

Fig 1.1 :A detailed illustration showing the anatomy of a robot with labeled components, including a mechanical structure, joints, sensors, actuators, control

1.6.1 Manipulator (Arm)

The manipulator is the robot's arm, often designed with several joints (or axes) to provide movement in different directions. The arm is responsible for the robot's movement and interaction with objects.

- **Joints/Links:** Robots typically have several links connected by joints (usually rotary or linear) to provide a range of motion.
- **Degrees of Freedom (DOF):** The number of independent movements the robot arm can make (e.g., 6-DOF means six axes of movement).

1.6.2 Joints and Links:

The manipulator of an industrial robot consists of a series of joints and links. Robot anatomy deals with the study of different joints and links and other aspects of the manipulator's physical construction. A robotic joint provides relative motion between two links of the robot. Each joint, oraxis, provides a certain degree-of-freedom (dof) of motion. In most of the cases, only one degree-of-freedom is associated with each joint. Therefore the robot's complexity can be classified according tothe total number of degrees-of-freedom they possess.

Each joint is connected to two links, an input link and an output link. Joint provides controlled relative movement between the input link and output link. A robotic link is the rigid component of the robot manipulator. Most of the robots are mounted upon a stationary base, such as the floor. From this base, a joint-link numbering scheme may be recognized as shown in Fig 1.2. The robotic base and its connection to the first joint are termed as link-0. The first joint in the sequence is joint-1. Link-0 is the input linkforjoint-1, whiletheoutput linkfromjoint-1 islink-1— which leadstojoint-2. Thus link1is, simultaneously, the output link for joint-1 and the input link for joint-2. This joint-link-numbering scheme is further followed for all joints and links in the robotic systems.

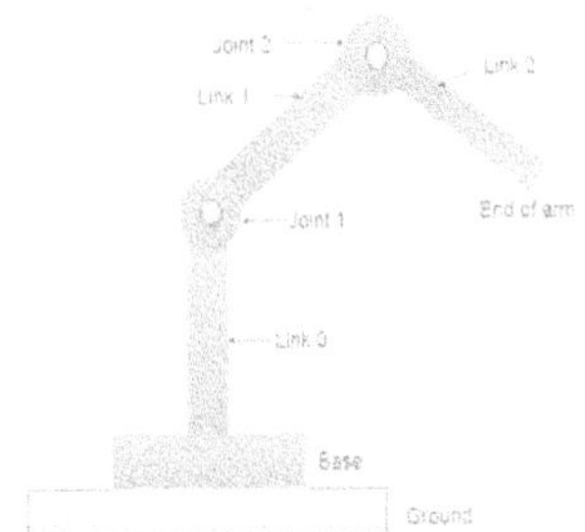

Fig.1.2: Joint-link scheme for robot manipulator

Nearly allindustrial robotshave mechanical jointsthatcan be classified into following five typesas shown in Figure 2.

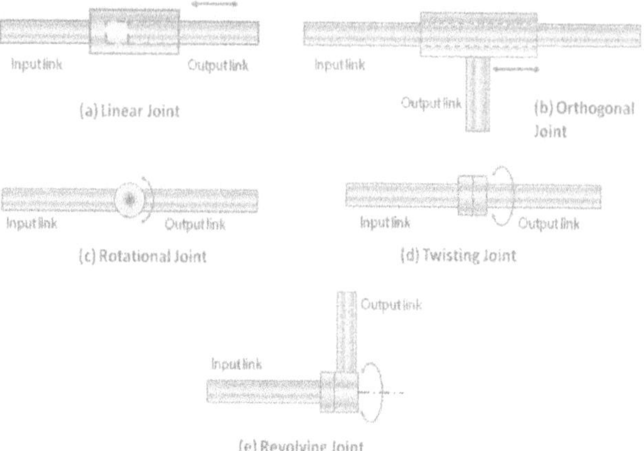

Fig.1.3: Types of Joints

a) Linear joint (type L joint)

The relative movement between the input link and the output link is a translational sliding motion, with the axes of the two links being parallel.

b) Orthogonal joint (type U joint)

This is also a translational sliding motion, but the input and output links are perpendicular toeach other during the movement.

c) Rotational joint (type R joint)

This type provides rotational relative motion, with the axis of rotation perpendicular to the axes of the input and output links.

d) Twisting joint (type T joint)

This joint also involves rotary motion, but the axis or rotation is parallel to the axes of the two links.

e) Revolving joint (type V-joint, V from the "v" in revolving)

In this type, axis of input link is parallel to the axis of rotation of the joint. However the axis of the output link is perpendicular to the axis of rotation.

1.6.3 End-Effector

The end-effector is the "hand" of the robot, used to interact with objects. The type of end-effector varies based on the robot's task.

- **Types of End-Effectors:**
  - **Grippers:** For grabbing and manipulating objects (commonly seen in industrial robots).
  - **Tools:** Welders, drills, or other tools that robots use in industrial applications.
  - **Suction Cups:** Used for delicate tasks like lifting fragile items.

1.6.4 Sensors

Sensors are essential for providing the robot with information about its environment, enabling it to make decisions.

- **Vision Sensors (Cameras):** Enable the robot to recognize objects, distances, and visual information.
- **Touch Sensors:** Allow the robot to detect physical contact and pressure.
- **Proximity Sensors:** Help the robot detect obstacles or nearby objects.
- **Force Sensors:** Measure the amount of force applied by the robot during tasks.
- **Infrared and Ultrasonic Sensors:** Used for detecting distances and avoiding obstacles.

1.6.5 Actuators

Actuators are the "muscles" of the robot, responsible for moving and controlling the robotic system. They convert electrical energy into mechanical motion.

- **Electric Motors:** Common in many robots to drive wheels, arms, or other moving parts.

- **Hydraulic Actuators:** Provide strong, precise movement for large industrial robots.
- **Pneumatic Actuators:** Use compressed air to power movements, often used for simple, repetitive tasks.

1.6.6 Control System (Controller)

The control system is the robot's "brain," where all decisions are made. It receives input from the sensors and sends commands to the actuators.

- **Microcontroller/CPU:** The main processing unit that executes the robot's programming.
- **Feedback Control:** Constant monitoring of sensor data to adjust movements and tasks in real-time.

Software Algorithms: Programs that determine how the robot behaves, often involving artificial intelligence (AI) for more complex tasks.

1.6.7 Power Supply

Robots need a power source to operate, which can vary depending on the size and type of robot.

- **Battery Packs:** Common in mobile robots, providing electrical power for movement and operation.
- **Electrical Outlet (Direct Power):** Some stationary robots are powered directly from a power grid.
- **Solar Panels:** Used in space robots or long-duration outdoor robots like the Mars rovers.

1.6.8 Mobility System (Locomotion)

For mobile robots, the mobility system includes components that allow the robot to move within its environment.

- **Wheeled Systems:** Simple and efficient for flat surfaces.
- **Legged Systems:** Provide versatility for uneven terrain or stair climbing (e.g., bipedal humanoid robots).
- **Tracked Systems:** Ideal for rugged environments (similar to tanks).
- **Flying Systems:** Use propellers or jets for drones or aerial robots.

1.6.9 Frame (Body)

The frame or body provides structural support to the robot. It houses all the internal components, including the sensors, actuators, and power source. The design of the frame depends on the specific function of the robot.

- **Lightweight Materials:** Often used to reduce energy consumption and increase agility.
- **Durability:** Materials like steel or aluminum are used in industrial robots for strength and longevity.

1.6.10 Communication Systems

Many robots require communication systems to interact with humans or other robots.

- **Wireless Modules:** Enable remote control or communication between robots and control centers.
- **Data Links:** Used to transmit information collected by the robot to a remote location (e.g., video feed from drones).

1.7 Robotic arm configurations:

For body and arm configurations, the reare many

different combinations possible for a three degree of freedom robot manipulator, comprising any of the five joint types. Common body and arm configurations are as follows.

1) Polar coordinate arm configuration

2) Cylindrical coordinate arm configuration

3) Cartesian coordinate arm configuration

4) Jointed arm configuration

1.7.1 Polar coordinate arm configuration (RRP):

The polar arm configuration is shown in the fig 1.4. It consists of a prismatic joint that can be raised or lowered about a horizontal revolute joint. The two links are mounted on a rotating base.These various joints provide the capability of moving the arm endpoint within a partial spherical space. Therefore it is called as Spherical coordinated configuration. This configuration allows manipulation of objects on the floor.

Drawbacks:

i. Low mechanical stiffness

ii. Complex construction

iii. Position accuracy decreases with the increasing radial stroke

Applications: Machining, spray painting

Example: Unimate 2000 series, MAKER110

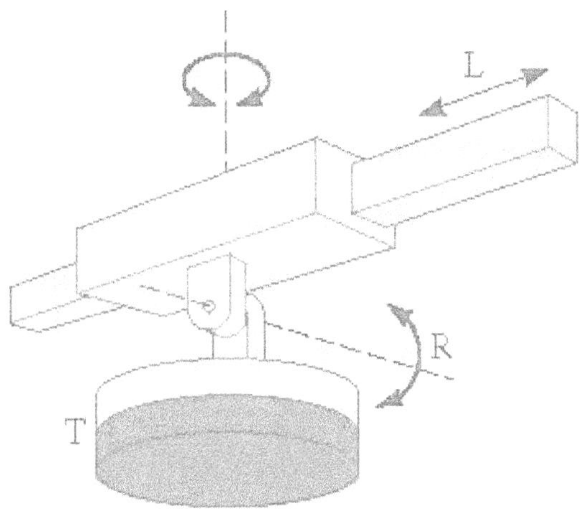

Fig 1.4: dof polar arm configuration

1.7.2 Cylindrical coordinate arm configuration (RPP):

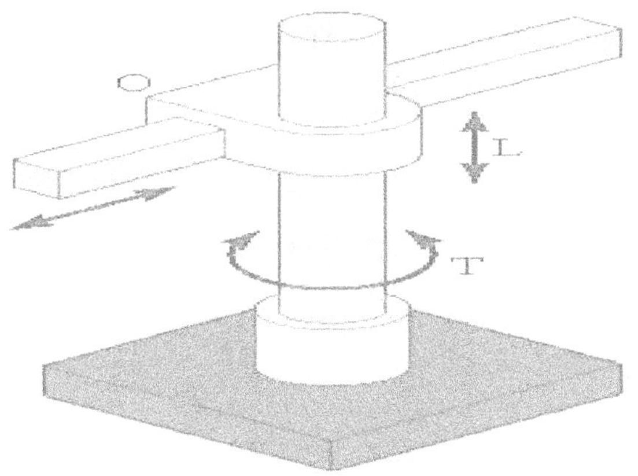

Fig 1.5 : dof cylindrical arm configuration

The cylindrical configuration uses two perpendicular prismatic joints and a revolute joint as shown in fig 1.5. This configuration uses a vertical column and a slide that can be moved up or down along the column. The robot armis attachedtothe slide, so that it can be moved radially with respect to column. By rotating the column, the robot is capable of achieving a workspace that approximates a cylinder. The cylindrical configuration offers good mechanical stiffness.

Drawback: Accuracy decreasesas the horizontal stroke increases.

Applications: suitable to access narrowhorizontal capabilities, hence used for machine loading operations. **Example**: GMF model M-1A.

1.7.3 Cartesian coordinate arm configuration (PPP):

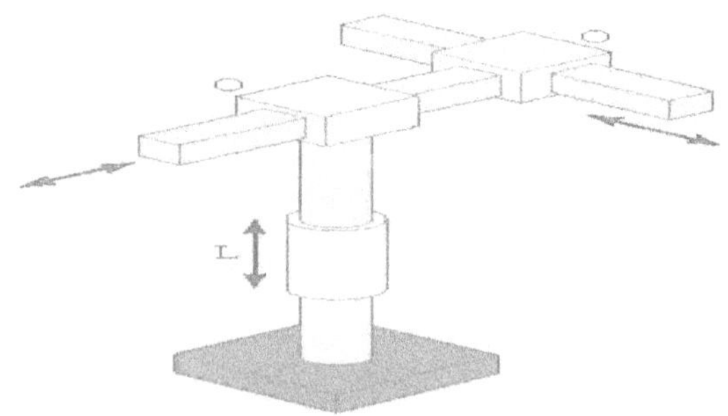

Fig 1.6: dof Cartesian arm configuration

From fig 1.6. Cartesian coordinate or rectangular coordinate configuration is constructed by three perpendicular slides, giving only linear motions along the three principal axes. It consists of three prismatic joints. The endpoints of the arm are capable of operating in a cuboidal space. Cartesian arm gives high precision and is easy to program.

Drawbacks:

- Limited manipulatability
- Low dexterity (not able to move quickly and easily)

Applications: use to lift and move heavy loads.

Examples: IBMRS-1

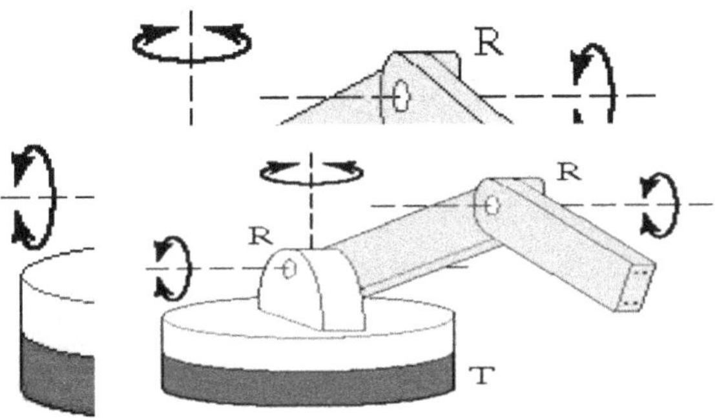

Fig 1.7: dof jointed arm configuration

From fig 1.7, jointed arm configurations are similar to that of human arm. It consists of two straight links, corresponding to human fore arm' and upper arm' with two rotary joint corresponding to the elbow and shoulder joints. These two are mounted on a vertical rotary table corresponding to human waist joint. The work volume is spherical. This structure is the most dexterous one. This configuration is very widely used.

Applications: Arc welding, Spray coating.

Example: **SCARA** robot (Selective compliance Assembly Robot Arm)

Its full form is Selective Compliance Assembly Robot Arm'. It is similar in construction to the jointed-arm robot, except the shoulder and elbow rotational axes are vertical. It means that the arm is very rigid in the vertical direction, but compliant in the horizontal direction.

The SCARA body and arm configuration typically does not use a separate wrist assembly. Its usual operative environment is for insertion type assembly operations where wrist joints are unnecessary. The other four body and arm configurations more or less follow the wrist joint configuration by deploying various combinations of rotary joints viz. type R and T.

1.7.4 Robot Wrist:

Wrist assembly is attached to end of arm. End effectors are attached to wrist assembly Function of wrist assembly is to orient end effectors. Body and arm determines global position of end effector It has three degrees of freedom:

- **Roll(R)** axis–involves rotation of the wrist mechanism about the arm axis.
- **Pitch(P)** axis – involves up ordown rotation of thewrist.

- **Yaw(Y)** axis – involves right or left rotation of the wrist.

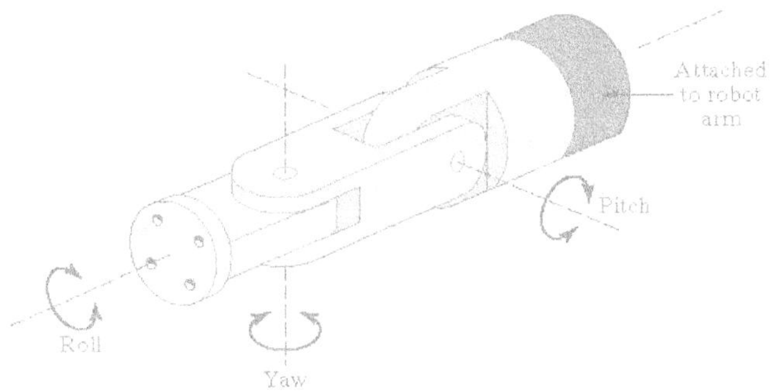

Fig 1.8: Robotic wrist

Robot wrist assembly consists of either two or three degrees of freedom. A typical three degree of freedom wrist joint is depicted in Fig 1.8: the roll joint is accomplished by use of a T joint; the pitchjoint is achieved byrecourse to an R joint; and the yawjoint, aright and left motion, is gained by deploying a second R joint. Care should be taken to avoid confusing pitch and yaw motions, as both utilize R joints.

1.7.5 Degree of freedom:

In mechanics, the degree of freedom (DOF) of a mechanical system is the number of independent parameters that define its configuration. It is the number of parameters that determine the state of a physical system and is important to the analysis of systems of bodiesin mechanical engineering, aeronautical engineering, robotics, and structural engineering.

The position and orientation of a rigid body inspace is defined by three components of translation and three components of rotation, which means that it has six degrees of freedom.

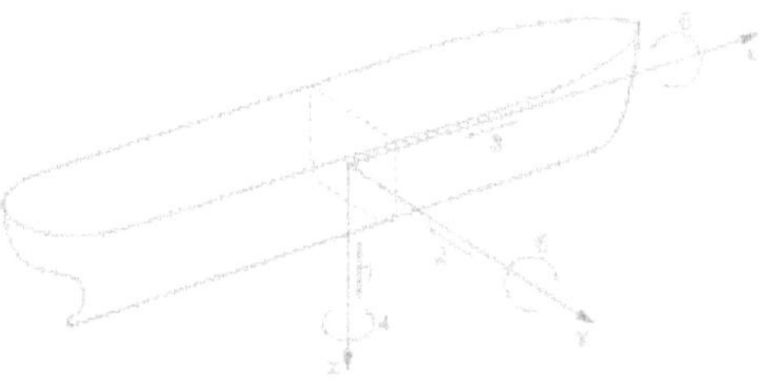

Fig 1.9: The six degrees off reedom of movement of a ship

The motion of a ship at sea has the six degrees of freedom of a rigid body, and is described as shown in fig 8.

Translation:

1. Movingup and down(heaving);

2. Movingleftand right(swaying);

3. Movingforward andbackward(surging);

Rotation:

1. Tiltsforwardandbackward(pitching);

2. Swivelsleftandright(yawing);

3. Pivots sideto side(rolling).

Fig 1.10: Attitude degrees of freedom for an airplane

From fig 1.10. The trajectory of an airplane in flight has three degrees of freedom and its attitude along the trajectory has three degrees of freedom, for a total of six degrees of freedom.

1.7.6 Robot work volume:

A space on which a robot can move and operate its wrist endis called as a work volume. It is also referred as thework envelopeand work space. For developing a better work volume, some of the physical characteristics of a robot should be considered such as:

- Theanatomyof variousrobots
- Themaximum valueformovingarobot joint
- Thesizeof therobot componentslike wrist, arm, and body

An industrial robot is a general purpose, programmable machine possessing certain anthropomorphic characteristics that is, human like characteristics that resemble the human physicalstructure, or allow the robot or espond to sensory signals in a manner hatis similar to humans. Such anthropomorphic characteristics include mechanical arms, used for various industry tasks, or sensory perceptive devices, such as sensors, which allow robots to communicate and interact with other machines and make simple decisions.

Both robots and numerical control are similar in that they seek to have co-ordinated control of multiple moving axes (called joints in robotics). Both use dedicated digital computers as controllers. Robots, however, are designed for a wider variety of tasks than numerical control. Typical applications include spot welding, material transfer (pick and place), machine loading, spray painting, and assembly. The general commercial and technological advantages of robot use are listed.

Table 1.1: General Commercial and Technological Advantages of Robot Use

Factor	Description
Work environment	Robots are ideal candidates formany harsh and dangerous working environments that are unsuitable for human personnel.
Work cycle	Robots have a level of consistency and repeatability in performing the work cycle, which cannot be attained by humans.
Reprogramming	Robot scan be reprogrammed and equipped as necessary to perform different work tasks one after another.
Computing systems	Robots use computers which allow them to be networked with other computers and machines, thus enabling computer integrated manufacturing.

1.8 Need for Automation:

Automation refers to the use of computers and other automated machinery for the execution of business-related tasks. Automated machinery may range from simple sensing devicesto robots and other sophisticated equipment. Automation of operations may encompass the automation of a single operation or the automation of an entire factory.

There are many different reasons to automate. Increased productivity is normally the major reason for many companies desiring a competitive advantage. Automation also offers low operational variability. Variability is directly related to quality and productivity. Other reasons to automate include the presence of a hazardous working environment and the highcost of human labor. Some businesses automate processes in order to reduce production time, increase manufacturing flexibility, reduce costs, eliminate human error, or make up for a labor shortage. Decisions associated with automation are usually concerned with some or all ofthese economic and social considerations.

1.8.1 Types of Automation:

Automation of production systems can be classified into three basic types:

1. Fixed automation (Hard Automation)

2. Programmable automation (Soft Automation)

3. Flexible automation.

1. **Fixed automation** (Hard automation): Fixed automation refers to the use of special purpose equipment to automate a fixed sequence of processing or assembly operations. Each of the operation in the sequence is usually simple, involving perhaps a plain linear or rotational motion or an uncomplicated combination of two. It is relatively difficult to accommodate changes in the product design. This is called hard automation.

Advantages*:*

   i. Low unit cost

   ii. Automated material handling

   iii. High production rate.

Disadvantages*:*

   i. High initial Investment

   ii. Relatively inflexiblein accommodating product changes.

1.8.2 Programmable automation: In programmable automation, the production equipment is designed with the capability to change the sequence of operations to accommodate different product configurations. The operation sequence is controlled by a program, which is a set of instructions coded. So, that they can be read and interpreted by the system. New programs can be prepared and entered into the equipment to produce new products.

Advantages:

iv. Flexible to deal with design variations.

v. Suitable for batch production.

Disadvantages:

i. High investment in general purpose equipment

ii. Lower production rate than fixed automation.

Example:

Numerical controlled machine tools, industrial robots and programmable logic controller.

1.8.3 Flexible Automation (Soft automation): Flexible automation is an extension of programmable automation. A flexible automation system is capable of producing a variety of parts with virtually no time lost for change overs from one part style to the next. There is no lost production time while reprogramming the system and altering the physical set up.

Advantages*:*

I.   Continuous production of variable mixtures of product.

II. Flexible to deal with product design variation.

Disadvantages*:*

I.   Medium production rate

II. High investment.

III. High unit cost relative to fixed automation.

Model Questions

Part A

1. Define the terms (i) Robots, (ii) Robotics
2. List out the power transmission devices.
3. State Asimov's laws of robotics.
4. Define the terms (i) Repeatability (ii) Compliance.
5. Explain the terms: Roll, Yaw and pitch of the wrist.
6. DefineDOF.
7. Define work volume, what is the physical characteristics that determine the work volume.
8. Distinguish between hard automation and flexible automation.
9. What is anend – effector?

Part B

1. With neat diagram, explain the anatomy of a robot and also define degrees off reedom.
2. Explain the robot classification based on the type of control employed.
3. With neat diagram, explain four common configurations.
4. (i) What is meant byDegrees Of Freedom (DOF) with respect to a robot.
   (ii) How do you determine that in arobot?
   (iii) How many DOFs are required in arobot?
   (iv) How cany ou increase the versatility of a robot in terms of DOF?
5. Describe spatial resolution, accuracy and repeatability of robot.
6. Briefly enumerate a chronology of historical events in the development of robotics.
7. State the Asimov's laws of robotics.
   What are the basic components of a
   robotic system? State the main
   function of each of the component.

Chapter 2

Sensor and Vision System

This chapter explores the different types of sensors used in robots and the importance of vision systems in modern robotic applications.In the field of robotics, sensors and vision systems play an integral role in enabling machines to perceive, interpret, and respond to their environments. These components are crucial for autonomous operations, real-time decision-making, and task precision.

2.1. Introduction to Sensors in Robotics

A sensor is a device that detects changes in the environment and converts them into signals that can be interpreted by the robot's control system. Sensors are the eyes, ears, and skin of a robot, providing information about its surroundings, location, and status. These data inputs are essential for performing tasks with accuracy, especially in unpredictable environments.

2.2 Types of Sensors

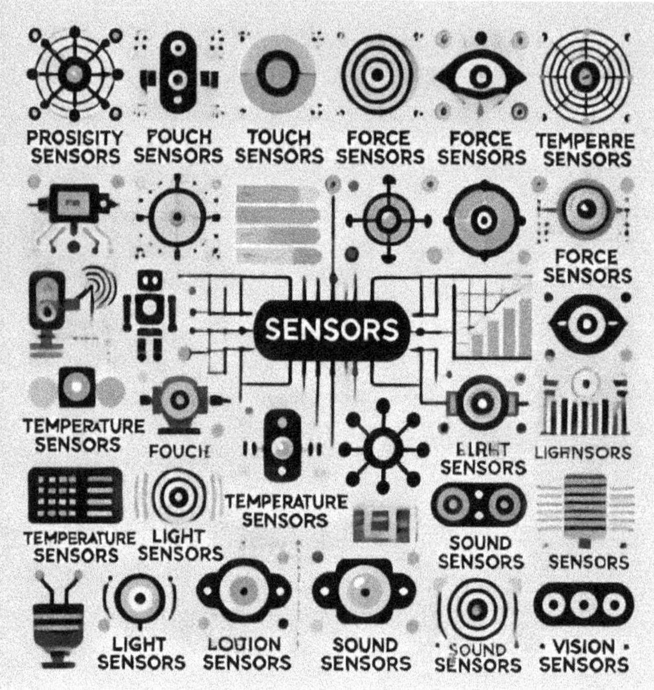

Fig 2.1 : An infographic showcasing different types of sensors used in robotics. The image includes representations of various sensors such as proximity sensors.

a) Proximity Sensors

- **Purpose:** Detect the presence or absence of an object within a certain range.

- **Examples:**

  - **Infrared Sensors:** Detect nearby objects using infrared light.

- o **Ultrasonic Sensors:** Use sound waves to measure the distance to an object.
- **Applications:** Obstacle detection, collision avoidance in mobile robots.

b) Touch Sensors (Tactile Sensors)

- **Purpose:** Provide feedback when the robot makes physical contact with an object or surface.
- **Examples:** Pressure-sensitive pads, resistive touchscreens.
- **Applications:** Gripping objects, assembly operations, detecting force.

c) Force Sensors

- **Purpose:** Measure the force exerted by or on the robot during tasks such as lifting, pushing, or assembling objects.
- **Applications:** Used in industrial robots to ensure precision in tasks like welding, drilling, or delicate part handling.

d) Temperature Sensors

- **Purpose:** Monitor changes in environmental or object temperature.
- **Examples:** Thermocouples, infrared temperature sensors.
- **Applications:** Useful in robots working in environments where heat is a critical factor, such as in manufacturing or electronics.

e) Light Sensors

- **Purpose:** Detect light levels and intensity in the robot's environment.
- **Example:** Photocells, LDRs (Light Dependent Resistors).
- **Applications:** Line-following robots, environmental monitoring, security robots.

f) Motion Sensors

- **Purpose:** Detect motion or changes in the robot's position.
- **Examples:** Gyroscopes, accelerometers.
- **Applications:** Used in autonomous drones, robotic arms for accurate positioning and stability control.

g) Sound Sensors

- **Purpose:** Detect sound waves to recognize audio signals or environmental noise.
- **Examples:** Microphones, piezoelectric sensors.
- **Applications:** Voice-controlled robots, human-robot interaction systems.

h) Vision Sensors

- **Purpose:** Provide visual feedback by capturing images or video for object recognition, navigation, and real-time decision-making.
- **Example:** Cameras (standard, infrared, thermal).

Applications: Explained in detail in the next section.

2.3 Transducers and sensors:

Transducer is a device that converts one type of physical variable (eg; force, temperature, velocity, flowrate etc) into another form. Generally we convert this to electrical voltages. There as on for this is that the converted signal is more convenient to use and evaluate.

Sensor is just used to sense the signals. Any transducer or sensor requires calibration inorder to be useful as a measuring device calibration is the procedure by which the relation between the measured variable and the converted output signal is established.

2.3.1 Types of transducers:

1. Analog Trancducers.

Provides a continuous signal such as electrical voltage or current as output.

2. Digital Trancducers:

Provides digital output signal in the form of status bits or series of pulses that can be counted. Output value represents the measured value. Digital trancducers are more easy to read the output and they offer high accuracy and more compatible with digital computer than analog based sensors.

2.3.2 Desirable features of Sensors:

1. Accuracy

Accuracy should be high. How close output to the true value is the accuracy of the device.

2. Precision

There should not be any variations in the sensed output over a period of time precision of the sensor should be high.

3. Operating Range

Sensor should have wide range of operation and should be accurate and precise over this entire range.

4. Speed of Response

Should be capable of responding to the changes in the sensed variable in minimum time.

5. Calibration

Sensor should be easy to calibrate time and trouble required to calibrate should be minimum. It should not require frequent recalibration.

6. Reliability

It should have high reliability. Frequent failure should not happen.

7. Cost and Ease of operation

Cost should be also was possible, installation, operation and maintenance should be easy and should not required skilled or highly trained persons.

Examples of Sensors:

a) Potentiometers

b) Thermocouples, thermistors.

c) Straingauge

d) Loadcell

e) Infraredsensors

f) LVDT

g) Pyrometers

h) Pizeoelectric devices

i) Pressure Transducers

j) Vision and voice sensors.

2.4 Definitions of Sensor Types:

Robotic Sensors:

Sensors are devices that detect changes in the environment (e.g., light, sound, temperature, or force) and convert them into signals that the robot's control system can interpret. These sensors allow the robot to perceive and interact with its surroundings. In robots, sensors function as their eyes, ears, and skin, enabling them to adapt to dynamic and unpredictable environments.

2.4.1 Static Sensors:

These are sensors that detect properties such as position, force, or pressure within a static environment. They are usually placed on the robot's body or stationary locations to detect certain environmental states or conditions. Static sensors can either require contact (e.g., pressure sensors) or function without physical contact (e.g., infrared sensors).

2.4.2 Contact Sensors:

These sensors require physical contact with an object or environment to detect specific changes or triggers. Examples include touch sensors, pressure sensors, and tactile sensors. These are vital for tasks like object manipulation, where the robot needs to feel the object it is interacting with.

2.4.3 Non-Contact Sensors:

These sensors detect the environment or objects without physical contact. They use technologies such as infrared, ultrasonic, or laser to measure distance, motion, or temperature. Examples include proximity sensors, light sensors, and temperature sensors, which help in identifying obstacles, monitoring surroundings, or tracking motion from a distance.

2.4.4 Environmental Sensors:

These sensors are used to detect changes in the external environment of the robot, such as temperature, humidity, or light intensity. They are crucial for adapting to changing environmental conditions and ensuring the robot operates efficiently in different climates or settings.

2.4.5 Non-Contact Environmental Sensors:

These are specialized environmental sensors that measure external conditions without requiring contact. Examples include light sensors, infrared sensors for detecting temperature, or ultrasonic sensors used for detecting obstacles at a distance.

Robotic Sensors are devices that enable robots to perceive and interact with their environment, mimicking human-like senses and capabilities. In certain applications, relying solely on workstation control using interlocks is inadequate. To perform tasks more effectively and autonomously, robots must possess sensory abilities such as vision, hand-eye coordination, touch, and hearing. These senses allow robots to interpret data from their surroundings, adapt to changes, and execute complex tasks. Robotic sensors can be classified into three main categories based on these sensory capabilities:

Vision Sensors: Provide robots with the ability to perceive and interpret visual information, enabling tasks such as object detection, recognition, and navigation.

Tactile Sensors (Touch): Allow robots to sense physical contact, texture, and force, enabling fine manipulation and object handling.

Auditory Sensors (Hearing): Help robots detect and interpret sound signals, often used in voice recognition and interaction with humans.

These sensors play a crucial role in enhancing robot performance and adaptability in dynamic environments.

The basic outline for Table 2.1: Advanced Sensor Technologies for Robotics, which lists several advanced sensor technologies commonly used in robotics:

Sensor Type	Description	Applications
Laser Range Finders (LIDAR)	Uses laser beams to measure distance to objects by calculating the time it takes for the light to bounce back. Provides high-resolution mapping of the surroundings.	Autonomous navigation, mapping, obstacle detection.
Ultrasonic Sensors	Emits ultrasonic waves and	Distance measurement,

	measures the time delay of the reflected signal to detect objects.	object avoidance, obstacle detection in mobile robots.
Infrared Sensors (IR)	Detects objects based on infrared light reflection. Useful for proximity sensing and object detection in various lighting conditions.	Proximity sensing, line-following robots, object detection in low-light conditions.
Force/Torque Sensors	Measures the force and torque applied to the robot's joints or end-effector, allowing for delicate manipulation and object handling.	Grasping, assembly tasks, precision handling, compliance control.
IMUs (Inertial Measurement Units)	Combines accelerometers and gyroscopes to measure the robot's orientation, acceleration, and angular velocity.	Motion control, balancing robots, stability in drones, and autonomous vehicles.

Pressure Sensors	Measures the amount of pressure applied to a surface, allowing robots to detect variations in force, useful for handling fragile objects.	Tactile sensing, pressure-sensitive grasping, touch-based feedback in manipulation tasks.
Cameras (RGB-D Cameras)	Captures RGB images along with depth information, enabling robots to understand 3D environments for vision-based tasks.	Object recognition, mapping, navigation, and hand-eye coordination.
Magnetic Sensors	Detects magnetic fields to measure the position, orientation, or proximity of objects with magnetic properties.	Precise position control, alignment, and navigation in magnetic environments.
Temperature Sensors	Measures changes in temperature to	Thermal monitoring in robotic systems,

	detect overheating or monitor environmental conditions.	hazardous material handling, or temperature-sensitive tasks.
Bio-inspired Sensors	Mimic biological systems like skin, muscles, or vision to enhance robot sensitivity and adaptability in various tasks.	Soft robotics, human-robot interaction, advanced manipulation.

This table provides an overview of the technologies used to equip robots with advanced sensory capabilities, helping them perform more complex and dynamic tasks in real-world environments.

An overview of various types of robotic sensors and their applications, including some examples:

2.5 Sensor Types:

1. **Range Sensor**:
   - **Description**: Measures the distance between the robot and objects in its environment.

- o **Application**: Useful for navigation, obstacle avoidance, and mapping.
- o **Example**: LIDAR, Ultrasonic sensors.

2. **Tactile Sensor**:
   - o **Description**: Senses touch, pressure, or force applied to the robot.
   - o **Application**: Enables robots to handle delicate objects, detect contact, or assess the grip.
   - o **Example**: Robotic fingertips or pressure-sensitive surfaces.

3. **Proximity Sensor**:
   - o **Description**: Detects the presence of objects near the robot without physical contact.
   - o **Application**: Commonly used for obstacle detection, navigation, and avoiding collisions.
   - o **Example**: Capacitive, inductive, and infrared proximity sensors.

4. **Optical or Infrared Light-Based Sensors**:
   - o **Description**: Use light or infrared waves to detect objects, their distance, or their surface characteristics.

- o **Application**: Object detection, navigation, or environmental mapping.
- o **Example**: Infrared sensors, light curtains, or optical encoders.

5. **Voice Sensors**:
   - o **Description**: Capture sound signals for speech recognition or audio-based interactions.
   - o **Application**: Enable robots to understand and respond to voice commands or sounds.
   - o **Example**: Microphones, voice-activated systems.

6. **Internal Sensors**:
   - o **Description**: Monitor the robot's internal state, such as battery levels, temperature, or motor status.
   - o **Application**: Ensures the robot's internal health and performance.
   - o **Example**: Temperature sensors, battery monitoring sensors.

7. **Position Sensor**:
   - o **Description**: Tracks the position or movement of the robot's components or the robot as a whole.

- o **Application**: Essential for precise movement, orientation, and control.
  - o **Example**: Encoders, potentiometers, GPS.

8. **Acceleration Sensors**:
   - o **Description**: Measure changes in velocity, enabling the robot to detect motion, tilt, or shock.
   - o **Application**: Used in self-balancing robots, fall detection, and motion tracking.
   - o **Example**: Accelerometers.

2.5.1 Applications of Sensors:

1. **Self-Balancing Robots**:
   - o **Sensors Used**: Accelerometers, gyroscopes, position sensors.
   - o **Purpose**: Maintain balance and stability during motion.

2. **Tilt-Mode Game Controllers**:
   - o **Sensors Used**: Accelerometers.
   - o **Purpose**: Detect tilt and orientation for motion-based gaming.

3. **Model Airplane Autopilot**:
   - o **Sensors Used**: Position sensors, accelerometers, gyroscopes.

- o **Purpose**: Maintain stability and follow preset flight paths.

4. **Alarm Systems**:
   - o **Sensors Used**: Proximity sensors, motion detectors, voice sensors.
   - o **Purpose**: Detect unauthorized movement or sounds and trigger an alert.

5. **Collision Detection**:
   - o **Sensors Used**: Proximity sensors, range sensors, tactile sensors.
   - o **Purpose**: Prevent robots from colliding with objects in their environment.

6. **Human Motion Monitoring**:
   - o **Sensors Used**: Acceleration sensors, tactile sensors.
   - o **Purpose**: Track and monitor human motion for rehabilitation or assistance systems.

7. **Leveling Sensor (Inclinometer)**:
   - o **Sensors Used**: Accelerometers.
   - o **Purpose**: Measure the tilt or angle of an object to maintain proper alignment.

8. **Vibration Detectors for Vibration Isolators**:
   - o **Sensors Used**: Vibration sensors, accelerometers.

- o **Purpose**: Detect and reduce vibrations to protect sensitive equipment.

9. **G-Force Detectors**:
   - o **Sensors Used**: Accelerometers.
   - o **Purpose**: Measure the forces acting on the robot during motion, useful in automotive or aerospace applications.

2.6 Axis of Acceleration:

- **Definition**: Refers to the directions in which an accelerometer measures acceleration. Commonly, accelerometers measure along one, two, or three axes (X, Y, Z), providing information about motion in different planes.
  - o **1-Axis**: Measures acceleration in a single direction.
  - o **2-Axis**: Measures acceleration in two perpendicular directions (e.g., X and Y).
  - o **3-Axis**: Measures acceleration in all three spatial dimensions (X, Y, Z), giving a full picture of the object's movement.

These sensor technologies play vital roles in enhancing the functionality, precision, and interaction of robots across a wide range of industries.

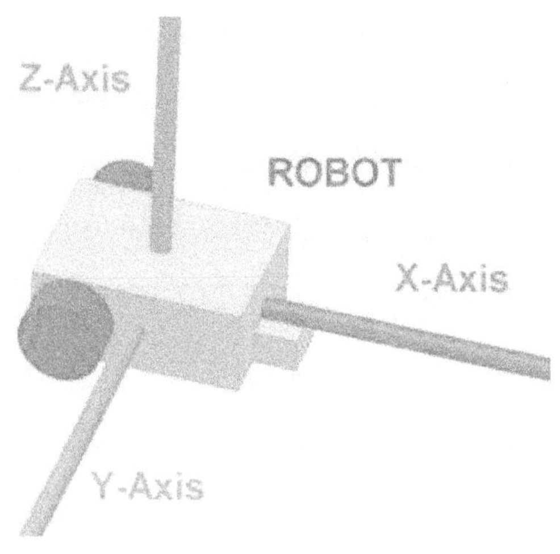

2.7 Understanding Gravity and Accelerometers in Robotics

Gravity as Acceleration:

- **Definition**: Gravity is the force that attracts objects towards the center of the Earth, causing them to accelerate at approximately $9.81 \, \text{m/s}^2 9.81 \, \text{m/s}^2 9.81 \text{m/s2}$ (this value is often denoted as ggg).

- **Impact on Robotics**: In robotics, particularly for bipedal robots, understanding gravity is crucial for maintaining balance. An accelerometer measures the acceleration forces acting on it, including gravitational acceleration.

2.7.1 How Accelerometers Work

- **Functionality**: Accelerometers can detect the orientation of a robot with respect to gravity by measuring the acceleration along multiple axes (typically X, Y, and Z).
    - If the accelerometer detects zero acceleration on the X and Y axes while experiencing the constant downward pull of gravity, it indicates that the robot is perfectly level.
- **2-Axis Accelerometer**:
    - A 2-axis accelerometer specifically measures acceleration in two dimensions (X and Y). This allows a biped robot to determine its tilt and adjust its posture accordingly to remain balanced.

2.7.2 Rated G of Accelerometers

- **Definition**: The term "rated G" refers to the maximum g-force the accelerometer can measure. For example, a **2g** accelerometer can measure accelerations up to $2 \times 9.81 \, \text{m/s}^2 2 \times 9.81 \,$ \text{m/s}^22×9.81m/s2.
- **Example**:

- o If a robot is moving upward at an acceleration of $1g1g1g$ (which is $9.81 \text{ m/s}29.81 \,, \text{m/s}\^{}29.81 \text{m/s2}$), the accelerometer will register $2g2g2g$ because it accounts for both the gravitational pull and the upward acceleration.

2.7.3 Selecting the Right Accelerometer

- **Common Ratings**:
  - o For most robotics applications, a **2g rating** is sufficient, meaning it can detect both the effects of gravity and reasonable motions or forces experienced by the robot.

- **Higher Ratings**:
  - o While it might be tempting to opt for an accelerometer with the highest rating available (e.g., 16g), such sensors can be less sensitive to minor changes in motion. This is due to their broader operational range, which can mask smaller accelerative changes.

- **Sensitivity vs. Vibration Interference**:
  - o **Lower Rated Sensors**: More sensitive to small changes in motion, which is ideal for fine-tuned applications like maintaining

balance in a biped robot. However, they may be more susceptible to interference from vibrations, which can lead to inaccurate readings.

- o **Higher Rated Sensors**: Less sensitive but can withstand larger forces without damage or saturation. They are more suited for applications where large accelerations are expected.

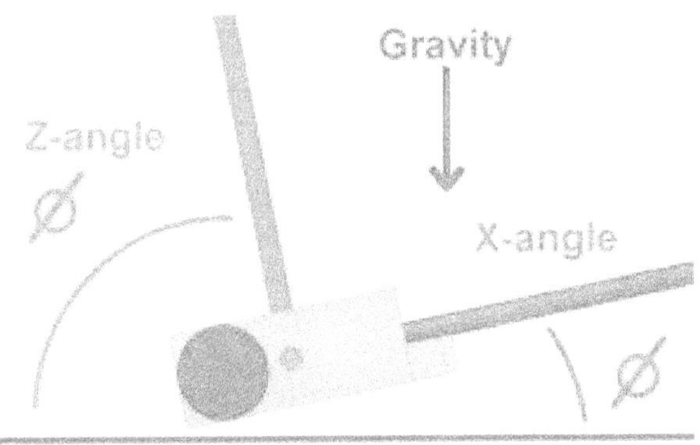

2.7.4 Calculating the Angle Using Accelerometer Data

In robotic applications, knowing the angle of tilt or orientation is crucial for stability and navigation. You can calculate the angle from the detected force using the following equation:

$$\text{angle} = \cos^{-1}\left(\frac{\text{sensor value} \times \text{conversion constant}}{-g}\right)$$

- **Variables**:
  - **sensor value**: The output from the accelerometer representing the acceleration detected on a specific axis.
  - **conversion constant**: A constant used to convert the raw sensor output into meaningful units, often related to the specific design of the accelerometer and its configuration.
  - **g**: The acceleration due to gravity (9.81 m/s^2), which is a constant.

2.7.5 Availability and Cost of Accelerometers

- **MEMS Accelerometers**:
  - Micro-Electro-Mechanical Systems (MEMS) accelerometers are widely available and cost-effective. They are commonly used in robotics due to their small size, low power consumption, and affordability.
- **Support Circuitry**:
  - While MEMS accelerometers can be very useful, they often require additional support

circuitry. This can be complex and may not be ideal for all applications.

- **Pre-assembled Modules**:
  - o Instead of building a custom setup, it's recommended to use pre-assembled accelerometer modules. For example, **Dimension Engineering** offers a plug-and-play dual-axis accelerometer that requires no additional circuitry, making it user-friendly.

- **Three-Axis Sensors**:
  - o Many sensors are now available in three-axis configurations, and some even include built-in rotation sensors, providing a comprehensive motion sensing solution.

2.7.6 Wiring Requirements

When wiring an accelerometer package, consider the following:

- **Power and Ground**:
  - o Every accelerometer will require a power line (often 3.3V or 5V) and a ground line.

- **Analog Output Pins**:
  - o There will be a separate analog output pin for each axis of acceleration (e.g., X, Y, and possibly Z for three-axis sensors).

- **Additional Features**:
    - ○ Some accelerometers may have extra features or pins for additional functionality. Always refer to the datasheet for specific wiring requirements and capabilities.

2.7.7 Additional Tips for Using Accelerometers

1. **Smoothing Output**:
    - ○ If you are placing an accelerometer on a mobile robot that experiences bumps, it may trigger the accelerometer unintentionally, leading to erratic readings.
    - ○ To smooth out the output, you can use a capacitor to average the readings over several hundred milliseconds. This can help filter out high-frequency noise from bumps.

2. **Enhancing Sensor Accuracy**:
    - ○ Reading tutorials on interpreting sensor data can significantly enhance the accuracy of your accelerometer readings. Proper calibration and understanding of how to interpret the data are critical for achieving reliable results.

2.7.8 Touch, Force, and Torque Sensors in Robotics

1. Tactile Sensors

- **Definition**: Tactile sensors are devices that measure physical interaction between an object and its environment. They are inspired by the biological sense of touch, allowing them to detect various stimuli, such as pressure, temperature, and mechanical deformation. Although tactile sensors can detect a range of sensations, they typically do not sense pain, which is a biological feature.

- **Applications**: Tactile sensors are widely used in:
    - **Robotics**: For robotic hands or grippers that can adapt their grip based on the object they are handling.
    - **Computer Hardware**: Touchscreens on mobile phones and tablets rely heavily on tactile sensing technology.
    - **Security Systems**: For touch-sensitive locks and alarm systems.

- **Types of Tactile Sensors**:
    - **Piezoresistive Sensors**: Change resistance in response to applied pressure.
    - **Piezoelectric Sensors**: Generate an electric charge in response to mechanical stress.

- **Capacitive Sensors**: Detect changes in capacitance caused by touch or pressure.
  - **Elasto-resistive Sensors**: Change resistance based on deformation (elasticity) under applied force.

2. Force Sensors (Force Transducers)

- **Definition**: Force sensors, also known as force transducers, are devices used to measure force or torque within a mechanical system. They are essential for applications where understanding the force exerted or torque applied is crucial for functionality and safety.
- **Types of Force Sensors**:
  - **Load Cells**: Specifically designed to measure force, typically in applications involving weights and loads. They convert a force into an electrical signal.
  - **Torque Cells**: Measured specifically for torque, they provide valuable data in rotating systems or applications where rotational force is applied.
- **Operation**: Force transducers operate based on various technologies, which may include:

- o **Strain Gauges**: These are widely used in load cells, where the deformation of a material under stress results in a change in resistance, which can be measured to determine the force applied.
  - o **Hydraulic or Pneumatic Systems**: Using fluid pressure to measure forces.
- **Importance**: Understanding the construction and operation of force transducers is essential to effectively integrate them into robotic systems. They allow for the monitoring of loads and stresses, enabling robots to interact safely and effectively with their environment.

An overview of the **Machine Vision System** in robotics, along with definitions for each component and key task:

2.8 Machine Vision System in Robotics

Machine vision is a vital technology in robotics that empowers robots to visually perceive and interpret their surroundings, enabling tasks such as navigation, object recognition, quality inspection, and automation. As robotics continues to evolve across industries, from manufacturing to healthcare, the ability of machines to "see" and make informed decisions based on visual data has become indispensable.

In this chapter, we will explore the core components of a machine vision system, their roles in the vision workflow, and how they contribute to building an intelligent robotic system. By understanding each element of a machine vision system, readers will gain insights into the integration of hardware and software in enabling robots to acquire, process, and analyze visual information.

Machine vision systems provide robots with the capability to interpret their surroundings visually, similar to human vision. These systems allow robots to:

- Recognize objects, patterns, or shapes.
- Measure dimensions and detect defects.
- Navigate through environments by understanding their spatial surroundings.
- Automate inspection processes in various industries.

The functionality of a machine vision system relies on a series of carefully coordinated components. Each component plays a crucial role in ensuring that images are accurately captured, processed, and analyzed in real-time.

The system then communicates with the robot's control mechanisms to guide its actions based on the visual input.

2.9 Components of a Machine Vision System

2.9.1 Image Acquisition Device (Camera)

At the heart of any machine vision system is the image acquisition device or **camera**. Cameras convert light from the scene into digital data that can be processed by the machine vision system. In robotics, different types of cameras are used based on the specific task and environment:

- **2D Cameras**: These cameras capture two-dimensional grayscale or color images. They are widely used in assembly lines, inspection systems, and quality control processes.
- **3D Cameras**: By using depth sensors, 3D cameras can capture spatial information, enabling robots to operate in environments where object positioning and distance are crucial.
- **Infrared Cameras**: These are used in conditions with low visibility or where the detection of heat signatures is necessary, such as in autonomous navigation or security systems.

The selection of the appropriate camera is critical in defining the resolution, frame rate, and data type needed for the application.

2.9.2 Optical System (Lenses)

Lenses determine the quality and clarity of the image by focusing light on the camera sensor. The lens selection is driven by factors such as:

- **Field of View**: The area of the scene that can be captured by the camera.
- **Depth of Field**: The range of distance over which the objects remain in focus.
- **Magnification**: The size of the object in the image relative to its actual size.

The lens ensures that the camera captures the required details with precision, affecting the robot's ability to accurately interpret the visual data.

2.9.3 Lighting

Lighting plays a critical role in ensuring image quality. Adequate **illumination** ensures that the features of the object or environment are captured with sufficient contrast, reducing errors in image processing. Common lighting techniques include:

- **Backlighting**: Illuminates the object from behind to highlight the edges or silhouette, often used for shape or edge detection.

- **Ring Lighting**: Provides even lighting around an object, eliminating shadows and ensuring uniform brightness.

- **Spot Lighting**: Directs light on specific regions to focus on key features of an object.

Well-designed lighting conditions enhance image capture, helping the machine vision system extract meaningful information more effectively.

2.9.4 Image Processing Hardware

Once the image is captured, the next step is processing the data. **Image processing hardware** often includes specialized processors that can handle complex computations in real time. The most common processing units are:

- **Graphics Processing Units (GPUs)**: Designed to process large amounts of image data in parallel, GPUs are ideal for tasks like pattern recognition, object detection, and feature extraction.

- **Field-Programmable Gate Arrays (FPGAs)**: Provide custom, high-speed processing of vision algorithms and are often used in industrial automation applications.

- **Vision Processing Units (VPUs)**: Dedicated processors for machine vision applications, often optimized for energy efficiency and real-time performance.

This hardware accelerates image processing, enabling robots to analyze images and make decisions instantaneously.

2.9.5 Vision Software

The core intelligence of the system lies in the **vision software**, where image data is analyzed and interpreted. Common software functions include:

- **Object Recognition**: Identifying specific objects or patterns in an image based on shape, color, or texture.

- **Edge Detection**: Detecting the boundaries of objects within an image, essential for positioning and alignment tasks.

- **Pattern Matching**: Comparing captured images with stored templates to identify defects or confirm object characteristics.

- **Feature Extraction**: Isolating key features such as size, position, or orientation of objects for further processing.

The software uses sophisticated algorithms and models to process images and transform raw data into actionable insights for the robot.

2.9.6 Frame Grabber

A **frame grabber** is an intermediate device responsible for capturing individual frames from a video stream and converting them into a format suitable for processing by the vision system. The frame grabber ensures that the vision system can capture high-speed image data without loss of quality, which is particularly important in industrial automation applications.

2.9.7 Control System (Interface)

The **control system** coordinates all aspects of the machine vision system, integrating the vision data with the robot's motion control. The control system handles the following:

- **Image Capture Trigger**: It signals the camera to capture images at precise moments.
- **Lighting Control**: Manages the timing and intensity of the illumination system.

- **Data Processing Coordination**: Ensures that processed image data is available for decision-making in real-time.

The control system serves as the central hub, linking the vision system with the robot's mechanical actions.

2.9.8 Communications Interface

Communication between the machine vision system and the robot controller is facilitated by **communications interfaces**. Common interfaces include:

- **Ethernet**: A high-speed network interface often used in industrial environments.
- **USB/RS-232**: Simple and widely available communication interfaces for lower data rates.
- **Fieldbus Protocols**: Specialized communication systems designed for real-time industrial automation.

These interfaces ensure that data flows seamlessly between the vision system and the robot, enabling the robot to respond to visual information in real-time.

2.10 Workflow of a Machine Vision System

The typical workflow in a machine vision system involves:

1. **Image Acquisition**: The camera captures images from the environment.

2. **Image Preprocessing**: Filters and enhancement techniques are applied to remove noise or improve image quality.

3. **Image Analysis**: Algorithms process the image to extract features, recognize objects, and measure parameters.

4. **Decision Making**: Based on the image analysis, the control system makes decisions, such as whether a product is defective or an object needs to be moved.

5. **Action**: The robot executes the corresponding action, such as picking up an object or adjusting its path.

2.11 Applications of Machine Vision in Robotics

Machine vision systems are widely applied across various industries:

- **Manufacturing**: For automated inspection, quality control, and assembly line processes.

- **Logistics**: In automated warehouses for identifying and sorting packages.

- **Healthcare**: Assisting in surgeries or monitoring patients with robotic systems.

- **Agriculture**: Monitoring crops or performing automated harvesting with the help of visual data.

2.12 Modern Trends

The field of machine vision in robotics has experienced significant advancements in recent years due to innovations in hardware, software, and artificial intelligence. These modern trends are transforming the capabilities of robots, enabling them to perform increasingly complex and precise tasks. This will explore the latest trends in machine vision systems for robotics and explain how these advancements are shaping the future of robotic vision.

2.12.1 Deep Learning for Image Recognition

Deep learning, a subset of artificial intelligence (AI), has revolutionized machine vision by enhancing the accuracy of image recognition systems. Traditional machine vision relied on manually coded algorithms to detect and classify objects, but deep learning uses **neural networks** to automatically learn features from large datasets of images. This approach offers significant improvements in:

- **Object Detection**: Robots can now recognize a wide range of objects, even in complex or cluttered environments.

- **Image Classification**: Deep learning models can categorize images with high accuracy, enabling robots to differentiate between similar objects.

- **Pattern Recognition**: Neural networks can detect subtle patterns in images, which is useful in fields like medical imaging and quality inspection.

Deep learning allows robots to adapt to new environments and perform tasks that require higher levels of visual understanding.

2.12.2 Edge Computing in Machine Vision

Edge computing refers to processing data locally on devices, such as cameras or sensors, rather than relying on cloud-based systems. This trend is gaining popularity in machine vision for robotics because it reduces latency and increases the speed of image processing. Key advantages of edge computing include:

- **Real-time Processing**: Robots can analyze visual data instantly, making it ideal for time-sensitive applications like autonomous vehicles and industrial automation.

- **Reduced Bandwidth**: By processing data locally, there is no need to send large amounts of image data to external servers, reducing network congestion.

- **Increased Security**: Sensitive data, such as video footage from surveillance robots, can be processed on-site, reducing the risk of cyberattacks during transmission.

Edge computing enhances the efficiency and responsiveness of machine vision systems, particularly in scenarios that require fast decision-making.

2.12.3 3D Vision and Depth Sensing

Traditional machine vision systems were limited to 2D imaging, but the rise of **3D vision** has enabled robots to perceive depth and interact with three-dimensional environments. Modern 3D vision systems use techniques like **stereoscopic cameras**, **time-of-flight (ToF)** sensors, and **structured light** to capture depth information. Applications of 3D vision include:

- **Robotic Grasping**: Robots equipped with 3D vision can identify the exact shape and orientation of objects, allowing for precise manipulation, such as in picking and placing items in manufacturing.

- **Autonomous Navigation**: Depth sensing helps robots avoid obstacles and map their surroundings, improving their ability to navigate complex environments.

- **Quality Inspection**: 3D vision can detect surface deformations, cracks, or misalignments in products, which are difficult to spot with 2D imaging.

With 3D vision, robots gain a more comprehensive understanding of their surroundings, expanding their functionality in both industrial and consumer applications.

2.12.4. Hyperspectral Imaging

Hyperspectral imaging is a cutting-edge technology that captures images across a wide range of wavelengths, far beyond the visible spectrum. By analyzing the spectral properties of objects, hyperspectral imaging allows robots to detect materials, chemical compositions, and even food freshness. This technology is particularly useful in:

- **Agriculture**: Robots equipped with hyperspectral cameras can monitor crop health, detect diseases, and determine the ripeness of fruits and vegetables.
- **Pharmaceuticals**: In the medical field, hyperspectral imaging can inspect pills for impurities or ensure consistent chemical compositions during drug production.
- **Environmental Monitoring**: Robots can use hyperspectral imaging to assess water quality, detect pollutants, or monitor air emissions.

Hyperspectral imaging adds an extra dimension to machine vision, allowing robots to see beyond the visible spectrum and apply advanced analytics in specialized industries.

2.12.5 AI-Powered Defect Detection

In industries such as manufacturing and quality control, defect detection is a critical task for machine vision systems. The introduction of **AI-powered defect detection** has drastically improved the accuracy and speed of identifying flaws in products. This trend utilizes:

- **Convolutional Neural Networks (CNNs)**: These deep learning models are designed to scan images for imperfections, such as scratches, dents, or color inconsistencies.

- **Self-learning Systems**: AI-driven defect detection systems can continuously improve by learning from past inspections, adjusting their criteria, and becoming more efficient over time.

- **Automated Labeling**: Modern machine vision systems can automatically label and categorize defects, reducing the need for human intervention.

By incorporating AI, robots can now detect minute defects that would have been missed by traditional vision systems, leading to higher-quality products and more reliable automation.

2.12.6 Augmented Reality (AR) for Machine Vision

Augmented Reality (AR) is being integrated into machine vision systems, providing robots and human operators with enhanced visual information by overlaying digital data on real-world images. In robotics, AR is used for:

- **Collaborative Robots (Cobots)**: AR allows human operators to visualize instructions or assembly guides directly on the objects they are working with, streamlining the collaboration between humans and robots.

- **Maintenance and Troubleshooting**: AR-enabled robots can provide real-time visual feedback on machine conditions, assisting technicians in diagnosing and fixing problems more efficiently.

- **Training and Simulation**: AR can create simulated environments for training robots, allowing developers to test vision systems in virtual scenarios before deploying them in the real world.

AR enriches the machine vision experience by merging digital insights with physical reality, making robot-human interaction more intuitive and efficient.

2.12.7 Vision-Guided Autonomous Systems

The demand for **autonomous robots** that can operate independently in dynamic environments is driving advancements in vision-guided systems. Autonomous robots rely on vision systems for:

- **Self-navigation**: Robots equipped with vision sensors can navigate without predefined paths, using real-time image data to make decisions and avoid obstacles. This is widely used in drones, delivery robots, and autonomous vehicles.

- **Target Identification**: In scenarios like warehousing or security, robots can use vision systems to identify specific objects or individuals and take appropriate actions, such as picking items or tracking movements.

- **Simultaneous Localization and Mapping (SLAM)**: SLAM technology, combined with vision systems, enables robots to build detailed maps of their surroundings and localize themselves within those maps. This is key for robotic exploration and autonomous delivery applications.

As autonomous systems evolve, machine vision will continue to play a central role in enabling robots to interact with and adapt to changing environments.

2.12.8 Cloud-Based Vision Systems

Cloud-based machine vision allows robots to offload image processing tasks to remote servers, leveraging the computational power of the cloud. This approach has several benefits:

- **Scalability**: Large amounts of image data can be processed quickly and efficiently without the need for expensive local hardware.

- **Collaboration**: Multiple robots can share data in real-time, enabling them to work together and enhance decision-making processes.

- **Advanced Analytics**: Cloud-based systems can integrate machine vision with other AI services, such as predictive analytics or machine learning models, improving the robot's overall intelligence.

Cloud-based machine vision is especially useful for applications that involve large-scale data processing, such as smart factories or smart cities.

2.12.9 High-Speed Vision Systems

Modern robotics increasingly demands **high-speed vision systems** capable of capturing and analyzing images in milliseconds. These systems are essential for high-speed industrial applications where robots need to react instantly, such as:

- **Assembly Line Automation**: Robots in fast-paced production lines must identify, grasp, and place objects quickly, often operating at speeds beyond human capabilities.

- **Sports Analytics**: Robots with high-speed vision can track the movement of athletes or objects (like balls) in real-time, providing instant feedback or performance analysis.

- **Autonomous Vehicles**: High-speed vision allows self-driving cars to detect and react to changes in traffic conditions immediately, ensuring safe and efficient driving.

By improving the speed of image capture and processing, high-speed vision systems enable robots to handle time-critical tasks with precision.

The modern trends in machine vision systems are driving significant improvements in the capabilities of robots, making them smarter, faster, and more versatile. From deep learning and edge computing to 3D vision and hyperspectral imaging, these innovations are reshaping industries and opening up new possibilities for robotic applications. As machine vision technology continues to evolve, the future promises even more sophisticated and intelligent robots capable of performing complex tasks in a wide variety of environments.

2.13 Evolution and Trends

2.13.1. Early Days of Machine Vision

Machine vision systems first emerged in the 1960s and 1970s when basic image processing techniques were developed for industrial automation. These early systems had limited processing power and could only perform simple tasks like:

- **Binary Image Processing**: Early vision systems operated on binary images (black and white), using thresholding to distinguish between objects and the background.
- **Edge Detection**: Basic algorithms like Sobel or Canny were used to detect edges in images, allowing the system to identify object boundaries.

- **Pattern Matching**: Early pattern matching techniques allowed robots to identify simple shapes or text based on pixel comparisons.

While these systems were groundbreaking at the time, they were limited in their applications and required controlled environments with consistent lighting and object positioning.

2.13.2. Rise of 2D Machine Vision

In the 1980s and 1990s, machine vision systems evolved with the ability to process **grayscale** and **color images**, expanding their usefulness in various industries. This era saw the development of:

- **Feature Extraction**: Algorithms could now extract key features like corners, lines, and textures from images, improving object recognition.

- **Template Matching**: Vision systems could match objects to pre-defined templates, enabling more accurate identification of parts in assembly lines.

- **Quality Inspection**: 2D vision systems were widely used in manufacturing for tasks like checking product dimensions, detecting defects, and verifying assembly completeness.

Despite these advancements, 2D vision was limited in understanding depth and could struggle in environments with varying lighting or occlusions.

2.13.3. Introduction of 3D Vision Systems

The early 2000s saw the emergence of **3D vision** technology, which allowed machines to perceive depth and volume in addition to flat images. Key innovations in this era included:

- **Stereoscopic Vision**: By using two or more cameras to capture images from different angles, vision systems could calculate depth information and create 3D models of objects.

- **Laser Scanning and Structured Light**: These techniques projected patterns (e.g., grids or dots) onto an object and analyzed distortions in the pattern to infer depth.

- **Time-of-Flight (ToF) Sensors**: ToF sensors measure the time it takes for light to bounce back from an object, allowing for precise distance measurements.

3D vision greatly expanded the range of applications for machine vision, enabling robots to perform more complex tasks like object manipulation, autonomous navigation, and inspection of irregularly shaped objects.

2.13.4. Intgration of Artificial Intelligence (AI)

The integration of AI, particularly **machine learning** and **deep learning**, marked a significant leap forward in the evolution of machine vision systems. Traditional vision algorithms relied on hand-crafted rules, which limited their flexibility and accuracy in complex environments. AI-driven vision systems, on the other hand, offered:

- **Self-Learning Capabilities**: Deep learning models, such as **Convolutional Neural Networks (CNNs)**, automatically learn features from large datasets, improving object recognition and classification.

- **Enhanced Object Detection**: AI-based vision systems can detect and classify objects in cluttered environments with much greater accuracy than traditional methods.

- **Real-Time Decision Making**: AI enables faster, more adaptive vision systems that can operate in dynamic, real-world conditions.

This evolution significantly improved the capabilities of robots in industries like autonomous driving, healthcare, and agriculture.

2.14 Modern Trends in Machine Vision Systems

As machine vision continues to evolve, several key trends are shaping the future of this technology:

2.14.1 AI-Driven Vision Systems

AI has become deeply embedded in modern machine vision systems. **Deep learning** models, such as YOLO (You Only Look Once) and SSD (Single Shot Multibox Detector), are now standard tools for object detection and classification. The benefits of AI-driven vision systems include:

- **Improved Accuracy**: Deep learning models outperform traditional algorithms in complex visual environments.

- **Adaptive Learning**: AI systems can continuously improve by learning from new data, making them more flexible in changing environments.

- **Predictive Analytics**: AI-enhanced vision systems can predict future states, such as potential defects in products, by analyzing visual patterns over time.

AI is transforming machine vision into a more intelligent, adaptable system capable of complex decision-making.

2.14.2 3D Vision and Depth Sensing

While 3D vision has been around for several decades, recent advancements have made it more accessible and accurate. Innovations like **LiDAR (Light Detection and Ranging)**, **structured light systems**, and **stereo vision** are enabling robots to perceive their environment in three dimensions with high precision. Key applications include:

- **Autonomous Vehicles**: 3D vision allows self-driving cars to detect and avoid obstacles, pedestrians, and other vehicles in real time.

- **Industrial Robots**: 3D vision systems help robots identify, grasp, and manipulate objects more effectively in manufacturing and logistics.

The combination of 3D vision with AI allows robots to understand the shape, orientation, and position of objects more accurately than ever before.

2.14.3 Edge Computing for Real-Time Processing

One of the most significant recent trends in machine vision is the shift towards **edge computing**. This trend involves performing data processing on the robot itself, rather than relying on cloud-based servers. The advantages of edge computing include:

- **Reduced Latency**: Image processing happens locally, allowing for real-time decision-making, which is critical for time-sensitive applications like autonomous drones or industrial automation.

- **Increased Privacy**: Sensitive data, such as video feeds, can be processed on-site, reducing the risk of data breaches during transmission.

- **Energy Efficiency**: Edge computing reduces the need for constant communication with external servers, lowering power consumption in robots.

Edge computing is particularly beneficial for applications requiring fast responses, such as robotic surgery, self-driving vehicles, and surveillance.

2.14.4 Hyperspectral Imaging

Hyperspectral imaging goes beyond the visible spectrum to capture a wide range of wavelengths, providing detailed information about an object's chemical composition and properties. This technology is gaining traction in sectors such as:

- **Agriculture**: Robots equipped with hyperspectral cameras can analyze crop health, detect diseases, and monitor soil conditions.

- **Healthcare**: Hyperspectral imaging enables early detection of diseases and conditions by analyzing the spectral characteristics of tissues.

- **Environmental Monitoring**: Hyperspectral systems can detect pollutants or monitor the health of ecosystems by analyzing the spectral properties of water, soil, and vegetation.

The ability to analyze objects at the molecular level offers new possibilities for precision agriculture, environmental conservation, and medical diagnostics.

2.14.5 Collaborative Robots (Cobots) and Vision Systems

Another emerging trend is the rise of **collaborative robots**, or **cobots**, which are designed to work alongside humans in shared environments. Machine vision is a key component of cobot functionality, enabling:

- **Safe Interaction**: Vision systems allow cobots to detect human presence and adjust their movements to avoid collisions.

- **Augmented Reality (AR)**: AR-enhanced vision systems can overlay digital information on the robot's workspace, guiding human operators during assembly or maintenance tasks.

- **Human-Robot Collaboration**: Vision systems help cobots interpret gestures, facial expressions, or spoken commands, facilitating more intuitive interaction between robots and humans.

Cobots are increasingly being used in industries such as manufacturing, healthcare, and logistics, where human-robot collaboration is essential.

2.15 Evolution of Machine Vision Hardware

While software has evolved dramatically, advancements in hardware have also played a critical role in the evolution of machine vision systems. Some key hardware trends include:

- **Higher-Resolution Cameras**: Modern cameras can capture images at resolutions far beyond those of early vision systems, providing more detailed information for analysis.
- **Improved Sensors**: Advances in sensor technology, such as CMOS and CCD sensors, have enabled faster and more accurate image capture.
- **Specialized Processors**: The development of GPUs (Graphics Processing Units) and TPUs (Tensor Processing Units) has accelerated the processing power available for real-time vision tasks.

These hardware improvements have enabled machine vision systems to handle more data and perform more complex calculations, opening up new possibilities for robotic applications.

The evolution of machine vision systems has been marked by continuous innovation, from the early days of basic image processing to the modern trends of AI-driven vision, 3D imaging, and edge computing. These advancements are transforming robotics, enabling machines to perform increasingly complex and precise tasks in industries ranging from manufacturing and healthcare to autonomous vehicles and agriculture. As machine vision technology continues to evolve, it will play an even more integral role in shaping the future of robotics and automation.

2.16 Emerging Applications

The emerging applications where machine vision is transforming industries, enhancing robotic capabilities, and enabling more sophisticated automation.

2.16.1. Autonomous Vehicles

One of the most prominent and rapidly growing applications of machine vision in robotics is in **autonomous vehicles**. Machine vision systems play a critical role in enabling vehicles to perceive their surroundings and make real-time decisions, ensuring safe and efficient navigation.

Environment Perception

Machine vision systems equipped with cameras, LiDAR, and radar allow autonomous vehicles to identify and classify objects like pedestrians, other vehicles, road signs, and obstacles. Key components include:

- **Object Detection and Recognition**: Using AI-powered models, the system can detect objects on the road and determine their type, size, and position.

- **Depth Estimation**: Through stereoscopic vision and LiDAR, autonomous vehicles can calculate the distance between the vehicle and surrounding objects, ensuring safe navigation.

- **Traffic Sign Recognition**: Vision systems identify and interpret traffic signs and signals, allowing the vehicle to obey traffic rules.

Real-Time Decision Making

Autonomous driving requires instant decision-making in dynamic environments. Vision systems enable this by processing large volumes of image data in real time and determining appropriate actions, such as lane changes, braking, and accelerating. Vision-powered **collision avoidance** systems are crucial for ensuring road safety.

2.16.2. Healthcare and Medical Robotics

Machine vision is revolutionizing healthcare by enabling **medical robotics** to assist in complex procedures, diagnostics, and patient care. These systems are being used in both surgery and diagnostic applications to improve precision and outcomes.

Robotic Surgery

In minimally invasive surgeries, machine vision systems enable robotic arms to perform delicate operations with greater precision than human hands. Vision systems assist in:

- **3D Image Guidance**: Surgeons use 3D vision to visualize internal organs in high detail, guiding robotic instruments with exceptional accuracy.

- **Tissue Identification**: Vision-based AI can distinguish between different types of tissue, ensuring that only the target areas are operated on.

- **Real-Time Monitoring**: During surgery, machine vision provides real-time feedback, allowing surgeons to monitor progress and adjust as needed.

Diagnostics and Imaging

Machine vision in diagnostics uses **hyperspectral imaging** and **AI-powered analysis** to identify early signs of disease from medical images (e.g., X-rays, MRIs, CT scans). These systems help in:

- **Early Detection**: Vision systems can detect abnormalities, such as tumors, at early stages by analyzing patterns and colors invisible to the human eye.

- **Non-Invasive Diagnostics**: Robotic vision systems enable non-invasive diagnostic procedures by analyzing external features such as skin conditions or eye health.

2.16.3 Agriculture and Precision Farming

Precision agriculture is one of the most promising emerging applications of machine vision in robotics. In this domain, vision systems enable robots and drones to monitor crops, optimize yield, and reduce the use of resources like water and fertilizers.

Crop Monitoring

Machine vision-equipped drones and robots are used to scan vast agricultural fields to monitor plant health, growth stages, and detect diseases or pests. Key features include:

- **Plant Health Analysis**: Using hyperspectral and multispectral imaging, vision systems can detect early signs of nutrient deficiencies or disease in crops.

- **Weed Detection**: Machine vision systems can distinguish between crops and weeds, allowing robots to target and remove weeds precisely without harming the crops.
- **Yield Prediction**: By analyzing plant growth patterns, vision systems help farmers predict crop yield, optimizing the harvest process.

Automated Harvesting

Robots equipped with advanced machine vision systems are being deployed to automate harvesting in agriculture. These robots:

- **Identify Ripe Produce**: Vision systems detect ripeness levels of fruits and vegetables, enabling the robot to pick them at the optimal time.
- **Precision Picking**: Machine vision ensures that only the desired crops are harvested while minimizing damage to the plants.
- **Efficient Sorting**: After harvesting, machine vision systems classify produce based on size, color, and quality, improving the efficiency of post-harvest processing.

2.16.4 Industrial Robotics and Quality Control

Machine vision continues to have a profound impact on industrial automation, particularly in areas like **quality control**, **assembly**, and **inspection**.

Automated Quality Inspection

Machine vision systems are widely used in manufacturing to ensure product quality by inspecting items for defects, irregularities, and compliance with specifications. Applications include:

- **Surface Inspection**: Vision systems detect imperfections such as scratches, cracks, or dents on product surfaces, especially in industries like electronics, automotive, and pharmaceuticals.

- **Dimensional Accuracy**: By measuring the dimensions of products using vision-guided systems, manufacturers can ensure that each item meets precise size specifications.

- **Pattern Recognition**: Machine vision helps identify faulty patterns, such as incorrect label placements, color mismatches, or missing components.

Vision-Guided Assembly

In complex assembly lines, machine vision systems guide robotic arms to ensure accurate component placement. These systems:

- **Identify Components**: Vision systems help robots differentiate between various parts and ensure correct orientation and positioning during assembly.

- **Adaptive Manufacturing**: Machine vision allows robots to adapt to different product types without manual reprogramming, facilitating the production of customized items or small-batch runs.

2.16. 5 Retail and E-Commerce

Machine vision systems are now playing a vital role in retail and e-commerce through the use of **automated checkout systems**, **inventory management**, and **customer analytics**.

Automated Checkout

Vision-based checkout systems are transforming retail by automating the purchasing process, eliminating the need for human cashiers. These systems:

- **Product Recognition**: Vision systems automatically recognize products placed in a shopping cart or on a checkout counter, calculating the total cost without the need for barcode scanning.

- **Fraud Detection**: Vision systems help prevent theft by monitoring shopper behavior and ensuring all items are accounted for before checkout.

Inventory Management

In warehouses and retail stores, machine vision-equipped robots or drones are being used to monitor inventory levels and organize stock efficiently. These systems:

- **Track Stock Levels**: By scanning shelves or bins, vision systems can detect when products are running low and automatically trigger restocking.

- **Barcode and QR Code Scanning**: Vision systems enable robots to scan barcodes or QR codes on products for identification, tracking, and sorting.

2.16.6 Security and Surveillance

Machine vision is increasingly being applied to **security and surveillance** systems, enabling more intelligent and automated monitoring.

Facial Recognition

Machine vision systems with facial recognition capabilities are being widely deployed in security, allowing for automated identification of individuals in public spaces, airports, and secure facilities. These systems:

- **Identify Known Individuals**: Facial recognition systems can match real-time images with a database of known individuals for access control or law enforcement purposes.

- **Monitor Public Spaces**: In surveillance settings, vision systems continuously scan crowds for suspicious activity, enhancing public safety.

Behavior Analysis

Advanced machine vision systems can analyze human behavior in real time to detect abnormal or suspicious activities. These systems:

- **Monitor Movements**: Vision systems detect and analyze unusual movements or behaviors, such as loitering or unauthorized access, and alert security personnel.

- **Crowd Management**: During large events, machine vision can monitor crowd density and movement patterns to prevent overcrowding or dangerous situations.

2.16.7. Environmental Monitoring and Sustainability

Machine vision systems are also emerging as key tools in environmental monitoring and **sustainability efforts**, helping to track and analyze natural resources.

Pollution Detection

Robots equipped with vision systems are being deployed to monitor air and water quality. For example:

- **Aerial Drones**: Vision-equipped drones can scan large areas of land or bodies of water to detect pollutants, such as oil spills or harmful algal blooms.

- **Microplastic Detection**: Machine vision systems are used to identify and quantify microplastics in water sources, aiding in pollution reduction efforts.

Wildlife Conservation

Machine vision is helping conservation efforts by monitoring wildlife populations and habitats:

- **Species Identification**: Vision systems can identify animal species from images or video footage, enabling researchers to track biodiversity.

- **Poaching Prevention**: Vision-enabled drones can patrol protected areas and detect poaching activities, sending real-time alerts to authorities.

Comparison of Techniques

Technique	Description	Pros	Cons
Template Matching	Matches objects to stored templates	Simple, effective for few models	Limited scalability
Structural Techniques	Analyzes relationships between features	Robust to variations	Complex implementation

2.17 Applications of Machine Vision in Robotics

Machine vision systems are integrated into robotics for various applications, enhancing automation and operational efficiency. Key applications include:

- **Inspection**: Automatically inspecting products for defects or quality assurance in manufacturing settings.

- **Orientation**: Determining the position and angle of objects to assist in tasks like robotic grasping.

- **Part Identification**: Recognizing and locating specific components in complex assemblies.

- **Location**: Identifying and navigating within environments (e.g., autonomous vehicles).

Specific Applications:

1. **Industrial Automation**:
   - Quality control in production lines using vision systems to detect defects in real time.
   - Automated sorting of products based on visual criteria.

2. **Healthcare**:
   - Analyzing medical images (e.g., X-rays, MRIs) to assist in diagnostics.
   - Automating tasks in laboratories, such as counting cells or analyzing samples.

3. **Agriculture**:
   - Crop monitoring and analysis to detect pests or diseases.
   - Automated harvesting systems that identify ripe fruits or vegetables.

4. **Autonomous Vehicles**:
   - Object detection and classification for safe navigation.
   - Lane and traffic sign recognition for driving assistance.

2.18 Future Improvements and Research

As technology advances, ongoing research aims to enhance machine vision systems, particularly in complex environments. Some potential areas for improvement include:

- **Advanced Algorithms**: Developing more sophisticated algorithms for better image processing, segmentation, and recognition.
- **Deep Learning**: Utilizing neural networks to improve object recognition accuracy and adaptability across various conditions.
- **Integration with IoT**: Enhancing machine vision systems with IoT connectivity for real-time data sharing and analysis.
- **Adaptive Learning**: Implementing systems that learn and improve from new data, allowing them to adapt to changing conditions and tasks.

2.18.1 Training the Vision System

Training a vision system is essential for enabling it to recognize and interact with objects accurately. The process involves programming the system with a dataset of known objects, extracting their features, and storing these values for comparison with unknown objects in operational scenarios.

Key Components of Vision System Training

1. Feature Extraction

Feature extraction refers to the process of identifying distinctive characteristics of objects in an image. Features can include:

- o **Shape**: Contours and edges that define the object's outline.
- o **Color**: Hue, saturation, and brightness values that represent the object's color.
- o **Texture**: Patterns or surface qualities that describe the feel or look of the object.
- **Techniques**: Common techniques for feature extraction include:
  - o **Edge Detection**: Identifying the boundaries of objects within an image using algorithms like the Canny edge detector.
  - o **Histogram Analysis**: Evaluating the color distribution in images using histograms to understand the color makeup of the object.
  - o **Texture Analysis**: Using methods like Gabor filters or Local Binary Patterns (LBP) to capture the texture characteristics.
- **Storage**: The extracted features are stored in a structured format (such as a database) for easy access and comparison during object recognition.

2. Physical Parameters

To achieve accurate and reliable recognition, the following physical parameters must be controlled during the training phase:

- **Camera Placement**:
    - The camera must be positioned at the optimal angle and distance to capture the object without distortion.
    - Calibration of the camera is often necessary to ensure consistent results.

- **Aperture Setting**:
    - Adjusting the aperture controls the amount of light entering the camera. This is crucial for obtaining clear images under various lighting conditions.
    - A wider aperture allows more light and can create a shallower depth of field, which may be beneficial for isolating objects.

- **Part Position**:
    - The object's position should be consistent to avoid variability in feature extraction.
    - Fixtures or mounts are often used to secure the objects during the training phase.

- **Lighting**:
  - o Proper lighting is vital for highlighting the features of the objects. This may involve:
    - **Uniform Lighting**: Reducing shadows and reflections for consistent image quality.
    - **Directed Lighting**: Enhancing specific features by using spotlights or backlighting techniques.

3. Simulation Conditions

- The training environment should closely mimic the actual conditions under which the vision system will operate. This includes:
  - o Using the same types of objects that the system will encounter in real scenarios.
  - o Replicating environmental factors such as background distractions, ambient light levels, and potential obstructions.

2.19 Robot Applications of Machine Vision

Machine vision significantly enhances the capabilities of robots, allowing them to perform a variety of tasks with improved accuracy and efficiency. These applications can be categorized into three primary areas: inspection, identification, and visual servoing/navigation.

2.19.1. Inspection

In inspection applications, the machine vision system plays a pivotal role in assessing the quality and integrity of manufactured products. The robot typically supports this process, which may involve moving products into the field of view of the vision system.

Objectives of Machine Vision Inspection

- **Detecting Surface Defects**: Identifying imperfections such as scratches, dents, or inconsistencies in the product surface.
- **Label Verification**: Ensuring that products are correctly labeled with accurate information, such as expiration dates or product codes.
- **Assembly Verification**: Confirming that all components of a product are present and correctly assembled, which is crucial in industries such as automotive and electronics.
- **Dimensional Accuracy**: Measuring physical dimensions (e.g., length, width, height) to ensure they meet specified tolerances.

Advantages of Automated Inspection

- **Consistency**: Machine vision systems provide uniform inspection results, eliminating the variability associated with human operators.
- **Speed**: Automated systems can perform inspections at much higher speeds than manual methods, significantly increasing production throughput.
- **100% Inspection**: Unlike manual inspections that may rely on sampling, machine vision can assess every item in a batch, reducing the risk of defects reaching customers.

Applications

- **Manufacturing**: Used for inline inspection of products on assembly lines to ensure quality control.
- **Food Industry**: Inspecting packaging for compliance with safety and labeling regulations.
- **Electronics**: Checking circuit boards for component placement and solder joint integrity.

2.19.2. Identification

Identification applications focus on recognizing and classifying objects, with the goal of determining the type, position, and orientation of each item. Unlike inspection, which typically results in a pass/fail outcome, identification often requires further decision-making.

Key Applications of Identification

- **Part Sorting**: Automatically categorizing parts based on characteristics such as size, shape, and color, often using robotic arms equipped with grippers.

- **Palletizing**: Arranging products on pallets for storage or transport, optimizing space and load distribution.

- **Depalletizing**: Removing items from pallets and preparing them for further processing or packaging.

- **Picking Parts**: Selecting specific components from a mixed batch based on real-time visual input to assemble products.

Importance of Identification

- Identification processes often follow inspection and are critical for automated systems to make informed decisions. For example:
  - In a warehouse setting, the vision system might identify the type of product being handled, allowing the robot to determine the appropriate action, such as sorting or packing.

Techniques Used

- **Pattern Recognition**: Algorithms such as neural networks or support vector machines (SVMs) are often employed to classify objects based on their features.

- **Template Matching**: Comparing an unknown object's features to stored templates of known objects to determine its identity.

2.19.3. Visual Servoing and Navigation

Visual servoing refers to the use of visual feedback to control the movement and positioning of robots. This capability allows robots to adjust their actions in real time based on the visual data received from cameras or other imaging sensors.

Applications of Visual Servoing

- **Robotic Manipulation**: Enabling robots to adjust their movements dynamically to align with the position of an object accurately.

- **Automated Guided Vehicles (AGVs)**: Using machine vision for navigation, allowing AGVs to move efficiently within a workspace, avoid obstacles, and follow predefined paths.

Benefits of Visual Servoing

- **Precision**: Enhances the accuracy of robotic movements by continuously adjusting based on visual input, which is critical in applications requiring high precision, such as surgical robots or micro-manipulators.
- **Flexibility**: Enables robots to adapt to dynamic environments and interact with objects of varying sizes and shapes. For instance:
  - In warehouses, robots can navigate around obstacles and dynamically adjust their paths based on real-time feedback.

Techniques Used

- **Control Algorithms**: Algorithms such as PID (Proportional-Integral-Derivative) controllers are commonly used to manage the robot's movements in response to visual feedback.
- **Depth Perception**: Utilizing stereo vision or depth sensors (like LiDAR) to understand the 3D position of objects and navigate accordingly.

2.20 Visual Servoing and Navigation in Robotics

Visual servoing and navigation represent a crucial application category in robotics where machine vision systems are utilized to direct the actions of robots based on real-time visual inputs. The primary objective is to guide the robot's movements to achieve specific tasks, leveraging visual feedback to enhance accuracy and adaptability.

Key Concepts

2.20.1. Visual Servoing

Visual servoing refers to the technique of using visual information from cameras or sensors to control a robot's motion. This can involve:

- **Position Control**: Directly guiding the robot's end effector (e.g., a robotic arm) to a specific position based on visual data.
- **Trajectory Control**: Planning and executing a path for the robot's movement toward a target object in its workspace.

Example of Visual Servoing

A common example of visual servoing is when a robot is programmed to grasp an object. The vision system identifies the object's position and orientation, allowing the robot to adjust its movements in real-time to accurately reach and grasp the object.

2.20.2. Navigational Control

Navigational control focuses on path planning and obstacle avoidance using visual data. This includes:

- **Automatic Path Planning**: Determining the most efficient route for a robot to travel while avoiding obstacles.
- **Collision Avoidance**: Using visual inputs to detect potential obstacles in the robot's path and adjust movements accordingly.

2.21 Applications of Visual Servoing and Navigation

2.21.1. Part Positioning

In industrial settings, visual servoing is often employed for precise part positioning. The vision system assists robots in:

- Accurately aligning parts for assembly.
- Correctly positioning components for welding or fastening.

2.21.2. Retrieving Parts from Conveyors

Robots equipped with vision systems can retrieve parts moving along conveyor belts. This involves:

- Identifying parts as they move.
- Adjusting the robot's trajectory to retrieve the parts smoothly and efficiently.

2.21.3. Assembly Operations

Visual servoing aids in automated assembly lines, where robots must position themselves accurately to assemble components. The vision system guides the robot's end effector to the correct location to join parts.

2.21.4. Bin Picking

Bin picking is a complex application involving the following steps:

- **Recognition**: The vision system identifies target parts within a bin, determining their orientation and position.
- **Grasp Planning**: The robot calculates an optimal position for its end effector to grasp the identified part, even when multiple items are overlapping.

The bin picking problem has been significantly advanced by research, particularly at institutions like the University of Rhode Island. Commercial solutions, such as:

- **I-Bot 1 System** by Object Recognition Systems, Inc.
- **BinVision** by General Electric, utilize sophisticated algorithms for effective bin picking.

2.21.5. Tracking in Continuous Arc Welding

In welding applications, visual servoing is essential for maintaining the correct welding path. The vision system can track the weld joint in real-time, allowing the robot to adjust its movement to ensure high-quality welds and prevent defects.

2.22 Challenges in Visual Servoing and Navigation

While visual servoing and navigation offer significant benefits, several challenges persist:

2.22.1. Dynamic Environments

Robots often operate in dynamic environments where objects can move or change unexpectedly. This variability can complicate real-time tracking and decision-making processes.

2.22.2. Complex Object Geometries

When dealing with complex or irregularly shaped objects, accurately determining their position and orientation can be challenging. Advanced algorithms are required to process visual data effectively.

2.22.3. Occlusions

In bin picking scenarios, parts may overlap or obscure each other, making it difficult for the vision system to identify individual components. Developing robust algorithms to handle occlusions is essential.

2.22.4. Lighting Conditions

Inconsistent lighting can adversely affect the quality of the visual data captured by the cameras. Effective lighting strategies are necessary to ensure reliable object recognition.

The training of vision systems and their integration into robotic applications are pivotal for automating processes across various industries. With a focus on inspection, identification, and visual servoing, these technologies drive efficiency, accuracy, and consistency in manufacturing, logistics, healthcare, and more. Visual servoing and navigational control are fundamental aspects of modern robotics, enhancing the capabilities of robots in various applications, from manufacturing to complex assembly tasks. By leveraging visual feedback, robots can adapt to their environments, improve precision, and automate intricate processes. As machine vision continues to evolve, advancements in artificial intelligence and machine learning are enhancing feature extraction and classification techniques, leading to more sophisticated and capable systems. These developments will further expand the range of applications, enabling automation solutions that can adapt to increasingly complex tasks and environments.

2.23 Vision Systems in Robotics

Vision systems are essential for robots to interact intelligently with the world. Unlike simpler sensors, vision systems allow robots to analyze complex visual data, identify objects, measure distances, and navigate spaces dynamically.

2.24 Future Trends in Sensors and Vision Systems

a) Artificial Intelligence (AI) in Vision

- AI and machine learning algorithms are improving the capabilities of vision systems, allowing robots to learn from visual data and improve their accuracy over time.

b) Advanced 3D Vision

- Advancements in 3D cameras and depth sensing technologies enable robots to better understand and interact with three-dimensional environments.

c) Bio-inspired Vision Systems

- Inspired by nature, researchers are developing vision systems that mimic biological eyes (e.g., insect vision), enabling robots to see in ways that are more adaptive and resilient to environmental changes.

-

d) Miniaturization of Sensors

- As technology evolves, sensors are becoming smaller, cheaper, and more efficient, allowing for greater mobility and flexibility in robot designs, especially in micro-robotics and nano-robotics.

Part A: Model Questions

1. What are the desirable features of sensors?

2. What are the essential requirements for success in robot vision?

3. Give one example of a velocity sensor.

4. Distinguish between tactile and non-tactile sensors. Give examples of each type.

5. Compare internal state and external state sensors.

Part B: Model Questions

1. What are the types of fiber optic sensors? Explain in detail how they work.

2. Explain robot machine vision with a suitable diagram.

3. With a neat sketch, explain ultrasonic proximity sensors.

4. Discuss the different sensors used in robotics.

5. What are the functions of a vision processor? What are the steps necessary in image processing?

6. Discuss various sensors used in robots for various applications.

Chapter 3

Grippers and Robot Dynamics

In robotic systems, grippers and robot dynamics are essential elements for handling and controlling objects. Grippers are the robot's "hands," designed to interact with the physical world, while robot dynamics govern the motion and forces applied by the robot during tasks. This chapter provides an in-depth exploration of various types of grippers, design considerations, and the fundamentals of robot dynamics, including different formulations used to model robotic motion.

3.1 Introduction of Grippers and Robot Dynamics

In robotics, an **end-effector** is the device located at the end of a robotic arm, specifically designed to interact with the environment. The exact nature of this device varies depending on the application of the robot.

In a strict sense, which originates from serial robotic manipulators, the end effector refers to the last link (or end) of the robot, where tools are attached. In a broader sense, an end effector can be defined as the part of a robot that interacts with the work environment.

It is important to note that this definition excludes the wheels of a mobile robot or the feet of a humanoid robot, as these components are part of the robot's mobility and not considered end effectors.

3.2 Considerations in Robot Gripper Selection and Design

Industrial robots utilize grippers as end effectors for picking up both raw and finished work parts. Effective grasping of objects is contingent upon proper gripper selection and design. Joseph F. Engelberger, often referred to as the "Father of Robotics," has outlined several key factors to consider in gripper selection and design:

- **Reachability:** The gripper must have the ability to reach the surface of a work part.
- **Size Variation:** The design must account for changes in work part size to ensure accurate positioning. During machining operations, the size of the work part may change, so the gripper must be adaptable enough to hold work parts of varying dimensions.
- **Minimizing Damage:** The gripper must not cause any distortions or scratches on fragile work parts.

- **Surface Area Coverage:** The gripper should be able to engage with a larger area of a work part, especially if it has various dimensions. This increases stability and control during positioning.

- **Grasping Contacts:** Designing the gripper with resilient pads can enhance grasping contacts with the work part. Additionally, using replaceable fingers allows the gripper to accommodate different work part sizes through interchangeable components.

Determining the necessary gripping force for a gripper to effectively pick up a work part is also challenging. Several significant factors must be considered to establish this gripping force:

- **Weight Consideration:** The weight of the work part must be factored in.

- **Center of Mass:** The gripper should be capable of grasping the work part consistently at its center of mass.

- **Robot Arm Movement:** The speed of the robot arm movement and the relationship between the direction of movement and the gripper's position on the work part should be evaluated.

- **Grip Mechanisms:** It is essential to determine whether friction or physical constriction aids in gripping the work part.
- **Coefficient of Friction:** Consideration must also be given to the coefficient of friction between the gripper and the work part.

3.3 Various Types of Artificial Gripper Mechanisms

Gripper mechanisms can be classified into the following major categories:

1. **Mechanical Finger Grippers**
   - These grippers use mechanical fingers to grasp objects.
   - **Subclassification:** Based on the method of actuation (e.g., pneumatic, hydraulic, or electric actuation).

2. **Vacuum and Magnetic Grippers**
   - These grippers utilize suction or magnetic forces to pick up objects.
   - **Subclassification:** Based on the type of force-exerting elements:
     - **Vacuum Grippers:** Use suction cups to create a vacuum and grip smooth, non-porous surfaces.

- **Magnetic Grippers:** Use magnetic forces to grip ferromagnetic materials.

3. **Universal Grippers**
   - o These are versatile grippers that can handle various object shapes and sizes.
   - o **Subclassification:** Includes:
     - **Inflatable Fingers:** Grippers that adapt their shape when inflated to grasp irregularly shaped objects.
     - **Soft Fingers:** Flexible grippers that conform to the shape of the object being grasped.
     - **Three-Fingered Grippers:** Designed with three fingers for stability and flexibility in grasping different objects.

4. **Adhesive Grippers**
   - o Grippers that use adhesive materials to grasp objects.
   - o **Characteristics:** They can conform to various shapes and provide a strong hold without damaging the work part.

5. **Hooks and Scoops**

- o Simple mechanical devices used for grasping or lifting.
- o **Examples:**
  - **Hooks:** Designed to catch or hold objects using a hooked shape.
  - **Scoops:** Used for lifting materials in bulk, such as sand or gravel.

3.4 Mechanical Finger Grippers

Mechanical finger grippers are designed to replicate the functionality of human fingers, allowing robots to grasp and manipulate objects. One common type of mechanical finger gripper is the **linkage gripper**.

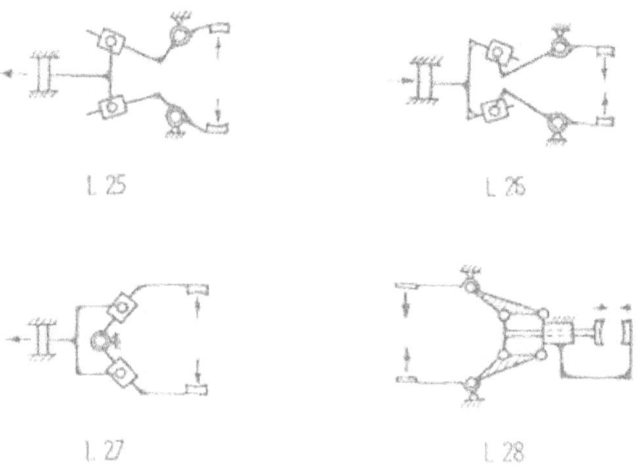

Fig 3.1: Linkage Grippers

(a) Linkage Grippers

- Linkage grippers utilize a system of interconnected links to perform gripping actions. Unlike other mechanisms, they do not rely on cams, screws, or gears for motion.

- **Mechanism:** The movement of the gripper is solely achieved through the relative motion of the links, which are attached to both the input actuator and the output gripping elements.

- **Design Considerations:**

    o **Kinematic Design:** A precise design of the linkage mechanism is crucial to ensure that the motion of the input actuator is effectively transformed into the desired gripping action at the output.

    o **Input-Output Relationship:** The arrangement of the links must be optimized to achieve a range of motion that allows for effective grasping of various objects, ensuring that the gripper can adapt to different shapes and sizes.

- **Applications:** Linkage grippers are often used in industrial settings for tasks such as assembly, packaging, and material handling, where precise and reliable gripping is required.

3.5 Gear and Rack Grippers

Gear and Rack Grippers utilize a mechanical design that incorporates gears and racks to facilitate gripping actions. This type of gripper is commonly used in robotics due to its ability to provide precise control and strong gripping force.

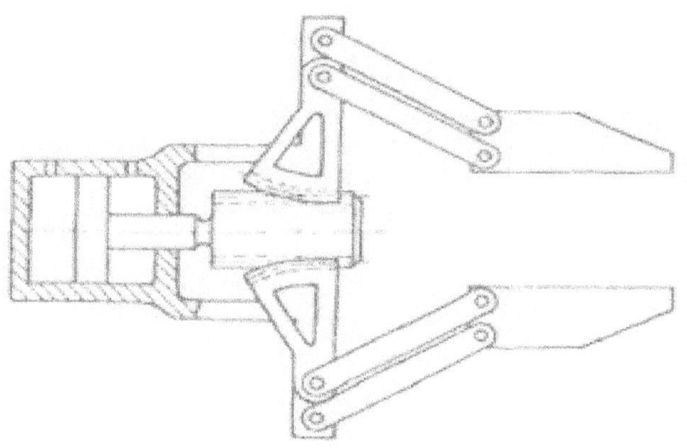

Fig 3.2: Gear and Rack Grippers

3.6 Mechanism Overview

- Gear and rack grippers operate by converting rotational motion from a motor or actuator into linear motion through a gear and rack system. This motion is then used to open and close the gripper fingers.

144

- **Components:**
  - **Gears:** A gear is a rotating machine part with teeth that meshes with another gear or a rack. The input gear, typically driven by a motor, rotates to create movement.
  - **Rack:** The rack is a linear component with teeth that interlocks with the gear. As the gear rotates, it moves the rack linearly, causing the connected links of the gripper to actuate.
- **Operational Mechanism:**
  - When the input gear is turned, its rotational motion is transmitted to the rack.
  - This movement of the rack causes the attached connecting links to move in a coordinated manner, resulting in the opening or closing of the gripper fingers.
  - The design ensures that the gripping action is both strong and reliable, allowing for effective manipulation of various objects.

Advantages:

- **Precision:** The gear mechanism allows for precise control of the gripper's position and force.

- **Force Multiplication:** The gear ratios can be designed to amplify the force applied by the actuator, enabling the gripper to handle heavier objects.

- **Compact Design:** Gear and rack systems can be compact, making them suitable for applications with limited space.

Applications:

Gear and rack grippers are widely used in industrial robotics, assembly lines, and packaging systems, where they require high precision and reliability in gripping various types of workpieces.

3.7 Cam-Actuated Grippers

Cam-Actuated Grippers utilize a cam mechanism to convert rotational motion into linear motion, enabling the gripping action of the fingers. This type of gripper is widely used in robotic applications due to its versatility and ability to create complex motion profiles.

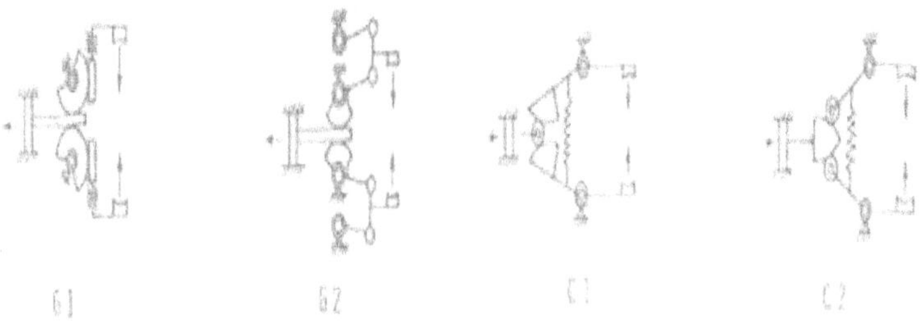

Fig 3.3: Cam-actuated Grippers

Mechanism Overview

- In cam-actuated grippers, the motion of a rotating cam drives the follower, which in turn moves the gripper fingers to perform a gripping or releasing action.

- **Components:**
    - **Cam:** A cam is a rotating element with a specially designed profile. As it rotates, its shape pushes against a follower.
    - **Follower:** The follower is a component that remains in contact with the cam. It moves in response to the cam's profile, converting the cam's rotational motion into linear motion.
    - **Gripper Fingers:** The fingers are attached to the follower. Their movement creates the gripping action necessary for manipulating objects.

- **Operational Mechanism:**
    - As the cam rotates, its profile engages with the follower, causing the follower to move in a reciprocating manner.
    - This movement translates to the gripper fingers opening or closing, allowing the robot to grasp or release objects.

- Different cam profiles can be used to achieve various motion characteristics, such as smooth transitions or rapid engagement.

3.8 Types of Cam Profiles:

1. **Constant Velocity Cams:** These produce a uniform motion, ensuring that the gripper fingers open and close at a consistent speed.

2. **Circular Arcs:** This profile provides smooth motion, making it ideal for applications requiring gentle handling of delicate objects.

3. **Harmonic Curves:** These are designed to create variable speeds, allowing for rapid engagement and slow release, which is beneficial for precise manipulation.

Advantages:

- **Versatility:** Cam-actuated grippers can be designed to achieve various gripping motions by simply changing the cam profile.

- **Precision Control:** The mechanism allows for precise control over the gripping force and motion, making them suitable for delicate tasks.

- **Compact Design:** Cam-actuated grippers can be compact, fitting into tight spaces while still providing effective gripping capability.

Applications:

Cam-actuated grippers are commonly used in assembly lines, packaging operations, and applications requiring precise handling of components, such as in the electronics and automotive industries.

3.9 Screw-Driven Grippers

Screw-Driven Grippers utilize the mechanical advantage of a screw mechanism to convert rotational motion into linear motion. This type of gripper is particularly effective for precise positioning and can apply significant gripping force.

Fig 3.4: Screw-driven Grippers

Mechanism Overview

- Screw-driven grippers operate by turning a screw, which in turn moves connecting links that control the gripping action of the output fingers.
- **Components:**

149

- **Screw:** The core component that converts rotational motion into linear movement. The screw can be powered by a motor, allowing for precise control.
- **Motor:** An electric motor is typically attached to the screw, enabling automated operation and precise control over the screw's rotation.
- **Connecting Links:** These links are attached to the screw and translate the screw's rotational motion into the opening and closing of the gripper fingers.
- **Gripper Fingers:** The fingers are connected to the end of the mechanism, which will either open or close to grasp or release objects.

- **Operational Mechanism:**
  - When the motor rotates the screw, it moves linearly along its axis.
  - This linear motion is transmitted through the connecting links, which causes the gripper fingers to move.

o The amount of rotation applied to the screw directly correlates with the opening or closing distance of the gripper fingers.

Advantages:

- **High Precision:** The screw mechanism allows for precise control over the gripping action, making it ideal for applications requiring exact positioning.

- **High Load Capacity:** Screw-driven grippers can generate significant gripping force, allowing them to handle heavy objects without slipping.

- **Simple Design:** The design is relatively straightforward, which can lead to easier maintenance and reliability.

Applications:

Screw-driven grippers are commonly used in applications requiring strong and precise gripping capabilities, such as:

- **Assembly Automation:** For securely holding components during assembly processes.

- **Material Handling:** In warehouses and factories for picking up and placing heavy items.

- **Robotic Surgery:** For tasks where delicate manipulation is required, such as in medical robotics.

- **Packaging Machines:** For gripping and positioning products on packaging lines.

3.10 Rope & Pulley Grippers

Rope & pulley grippers utilize a system of ropes and pulleys to achieve gripping actions through the winding and unwinding motion of the rope. This mechanism is typically driven by a motor, which allows for precise control of the gripper's movements.

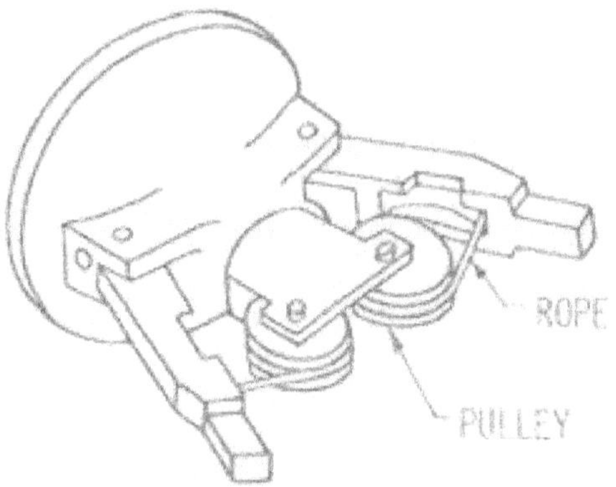

Fig 3.5: Rope & Pulley Grippers

Mechanism:

- **Motor Activation**: A motor is connected to a pulley system, which rotates to wind or unwind the rope attached to the gripper.

- **Connecting Linkage**: The rope is connected to the gripper fingers through a series of linkages. As the motor turns the pulley, the rope is either pulled (wound) or released (unwound).

- **Gripper Motion**: Winding the rope causes the gripper fingers to close or grip an object, while unwinding releases the grip. The movement is typically linear and can be designed to provide varying degrees of gripping force depending on the tension applied to the rope.

Advantages:

1. **Simplicity**: The rope and pulley system is straightforward and easy to understand, making it simpler to design and implement.
2. **Lightweight**: The use of rope instead of solid components reduces the weight of the gripper, which can be beneficial in applications where minimizing mass is crucial.
3. **Flexibility**: Rope & pulley systems can be adapted to different gripper shapes and sizes, allowing for versatility in handling various objects.
4. **Controlled Motion**: The motor-driven mechanism allows for precise control of the gripping action, enabling delicate handling of fragile items.

Applications:

- **Material Handling**: Commonly used in automated systems for picking and placing materials in warehouses or factories.

- **Robotic Arms**: Often integrated into robotic arms for tasks requiring precise gripping and manipulation of objects, especially in assembly lines.

- **Service Robots**: Employed in service robots that need to handle items carefully, such as in healthcare or hospitality industries.

Operational Principles:

- The motor's rotation is controlled by a feedback system, which may include sensors to monitor the position of the gripper fingers and adjust the motor's speed and direction accordingly.

- The tension in the rope can be adjusted to accommodate different sizes and weights of objects, ensuring a secure grip without causing damage.

3.11 Vacuum Grippers

Vacuum grippers use suction to lift and hold non-ferrous objects, especially those with flat and smooth surfaces. These grippers typically consist of vacuum cups or pads that create a negative pressure to securely attach to the object being handled.

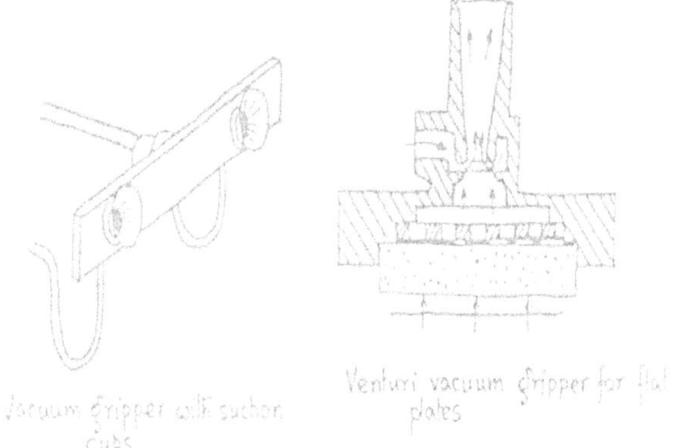

Fig 3.6: Vacuum Grippers

Mechanism:

- **Vacuum Generation**: A vacuum pump or venturi system generates negative pressure inside the suction cup. When the cup is pressed against an object, the air is evacuated, creating a vacuum that holds the cup to the surface.

- **Sealing**: The rubber-like material of the vacuum cup forms a seal against the object's surface, preventing air from entering and maintaining the vacuum.

- **Lifting and Releasing**: To lift an object, the vacuum is created and maintained until the object is raised. To release, the vacuum is released by allowing air to enter the cup, breaking the seal and letting go of the object.

Advantages:

1. **Gentle Handling**: Vacuum grippers can securely hold fragile or delicate objects without causing damage, making them ideal for sensitive materials.

2. **Speed**: They can quickly pick up and release items, increasing efficiency in automated processes.

3. **Adaptability**: Standard vacuum cups can be easily replaced or adjusted to accommodate different object shapes and sizes.

4. **No Mechanical Contact**: Since they rely on suction rather than mechanical gripping, there is less wear and tear on both the gripper and the object being handled.

Limitations:

- **Surface Requirements**: Vacuum grippers are most effective on flat and smooth surfaces; they are not suitable for curved, porous, or textured surfaces or objects with holes.

- **Weight Limitations**: The lifting capacity is limited to the strength of the vacuum generated, making them unsuitable for very heavy objects unless multiple cups are used.

Applications:

- **Packaging and Palletizing**: Commonly used in the packaging industry to lift and place products onto conveyor belts or pallets.

- **Material Handling**: Widely used in manufacturing environments to move glass, metal sheets, and other non-ferrous materials.

- **Assembly Lines**: Employed in assembly line applications where speed and precision are crucial, such as in electronics and automotive industries.

- **Robotic Systems**: Often integrated into robotic arms for applications requiring efficient handling of flat or smooth-surfaced components.

3.12 Magnetic Grippers

Magnetic grippers are specialized end-effectors designed to handle ferrous materials by utilizing magnetic forces. They are commonly used in industrial applications where materials such as steel plates or other ferromagnetic items need to be moved or manipulated.

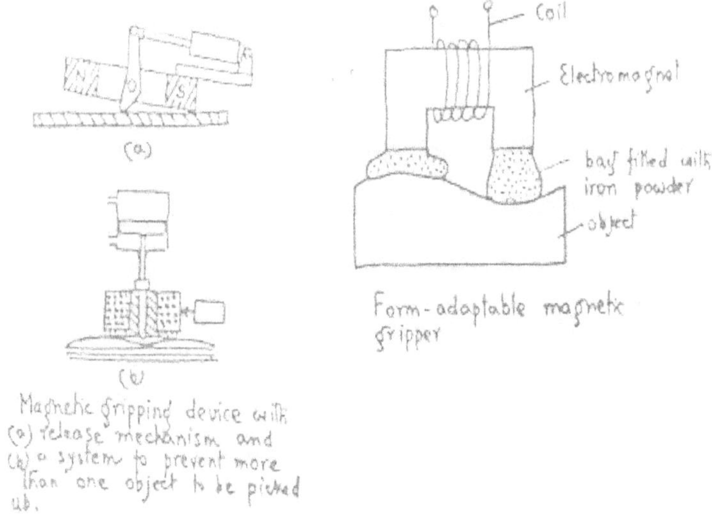

Fig 3.7: Magnetic Grippers

Mechanism:

- **Magnetic Head Construction**: The magnetic gripper consists of a ferromagnetic core surrounded by conducting coils. When an electric current flows through these coils, it generates a magnetic field, turning the core into a magnet.

- **Attraction**: The magnetic field attracts ferrous materials, securely holding them in place. The strength of the magnetic grip can be adjusted by varying the current supplied to the coils.

- **Releasing Objects**: To release the object, the current is turned off, causing the magnetic field to dissipate, which allows the ferrous material to be released.

Advantages:

1. **Secure Holding**: Magnetic grippers provide a strong and reliable grip on ferrous materials, reducing the risk of dropping or mishandling.

2. **No Mechanical Wear**: Unlike traditional mechanical grippers, magnetic grippers have no physical contact with the object during gripping, resulting in minimal wear and tear.

3. **Quick Release**: The ability to quickly switch on and off the magnetic field allows for rapid handling of materials.

4. **Adaptability**: They can be used on various shapes and sizes of ferrous materials without the need for adjustments or specific gripping designs.

Limitations:

- **Ferrous Materials Only**: Magnetic grippers are limited to handling ferrous materials; they cannot grip non-ferrous items like aluminum, copper, or plastics.

- **Surface Finish**: The effectiveness of magnetic gripping can be affected by the surface finish of the material; rust, dirt, or coatings can reduce the grip strength.

- **Weight Considerations**: The weight that can be lifted is determined by the magnetic force, which may not be suitable for very heavy objects unless multiple magnets are used.

Applications:

- **Metal Fabrication**: Widely used in metal fabrication industries for handling steel sheets, bars, and plates.

- **Assembly Lines**: Commonly found in automotive and manufacturing assembly lines to move metal parts quickly and efficiently.

- **Robotics**: Integrated into robotic systems for tasks involving ferrous components, such as welding or machining.

- **Warehouse and Logistics**: Used in material handling systems for quickly moving metal products and components in warehouses and distribution centers.

3.13 Universal Grippers: Inflatable Grippers

Inflatable grippers are a type of versatile gripper designed to handle irregularly shaped or delicate objects. They utilize flexible bags or bellows that can conform to the shape of the object being gripped, allowing for even distribution of force without causing damage.

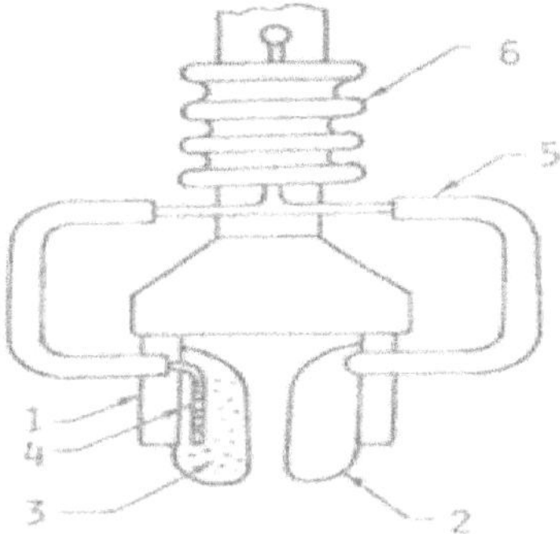

Fig 3.8: Inflatable Grippers

Mechanism:

- **Initial Position**: In the starting position, the inflatable gripper's levers are opened, and the bellows are in a compressed state due to gas pressure within the bags.

- **Gripping Action**: When an object is placed against the bags, even slight pressure is enough to depress the bag walls, allowing them to surround the object. The bellows expand to conform to the shape of the object.

- **Securing the Grip**: Once the object is adequately surrounded, the pressure in the bags is reduced using a diaphragm device, vacuum pump, or bellows mechanism. This hardens the bags without altering their shape, effectively securing the object in place.
- **Releasing the Object**: To release the object, the process is reversed. The pressure in the bags is re-increased, allowing the gripper to detach from the object.

Advantages:

1. **Gentle Handling**: Inflatable grippers distribute pressure evenly, making them suitable for delicate and irregularly shaped objects without risk of damage.
2. **Versatility**: They can adapt to a wide range of object shapes and sizes, making them highly versatile in different applications.
3. **Lightweight**: These grippers tend to be lightweight and can be easily integrated into robotic systems.
4. **Simple Design**: The mechanism is relatively simple and can be designed with fewer moving parts compared to traditional grippers.

Limitations:

- **Air Leakage**: Potential for air leakage can reduce gripping force and reliability over time.

- **Limited Load Capacity**: The gripping force may not be sufficient for heavier or denser objects.

- **Dependence on Pressure**: The effectiveness of the grip depends on maintaining the correct internal pressure in the bags.

Applications:

- **Food Handling**: Commonly used in the food industry for picking and placing delicate items like fruits and vegetables without bruising.

- **Packaging**: Utilized in packaging operations for handling fragile items like glass bottles or boxes.

- **Assembly Lines**: Ideal for assembling components that require a gentle touch, such as electronics or soft materials.

- **Medical Applications**: Employed in medical settings for handling sensitive items, including surgical instruments or medical devices.

3.14 Soft Grippers

Soft grippers are a type of robotic gripper designed to handle objects with varying shapes and sizes by conforming to their surfaces. These grippers are typically made from flexible materials and consist of multiple links and pulleys, allowing them to provide a gentle and uniform grip.

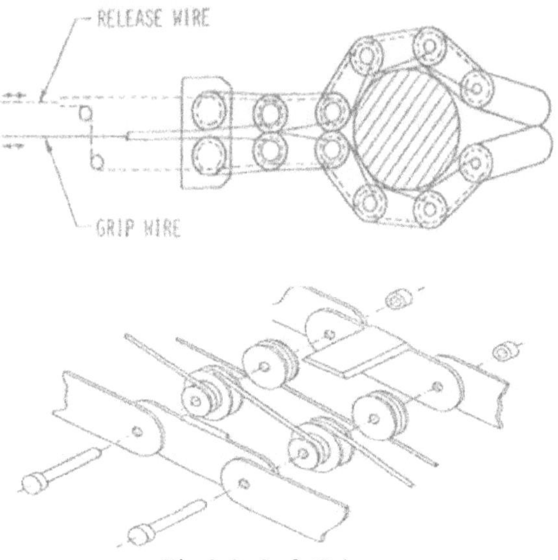

Fig 3.9: Soft Grippers

Mechanism:

- **Structure**: Soft grippers consist of a series of flexible links connected through a system of pulleys. They are often constructed from soft materials, such as silicone or rubber, which can deform and adapt to the shapes of objects.

- **Actuation**: The gripper is actuated using wires that pull on the links, allowing the gripper to close around an object. This pulling action causes the soft materials to flex and conform to the shape of the object.

- **Gripping Action**: When the wires are tensioned, the gripper's fingers wrap around the object, distributing the gripping force evenly across its surface. This helps to minimize the risk of damaging delicate items.

- **Release Mechanism**: To release the object, the tension in the wires is decreased, allowing the gripper to open up and let go of the object.

Advantages:

1. **Gentle Handling**: Soft grippers can handle fragile and irregularly shaped objects without causing damage, making them ideal for sensitive materials.

2. **Adaptability**: They can easily conform to a wide variety of shapes and sizes, enhancing their versatility in various applications.

3. **Uniform Pressure Distribution**: The design allows for uniform pressure across the gripping surface, reducing the risk of crushing or marking the object.

4. **Lightweight Design**: Soft grippers are typically lightweight, which can enhance the efficiency of robotic systems.

Limitations:

- **Limited Load Capacity**: Soft grippers may not be suitable for handling very heavy or rigid objects due to their flexible nature.

- **Durability**: Over time, the materials used may wear out or become damaged, especially when handling sharp or abrasive items.

- **Complex Control**: The actuation and control systems can be more complex compared to rigid grippers, requiring advanced algorithms for precise movement.

Applications:

- **Food Industry**: Frequently used for picking and placing soft or fragile food items like fruits, vegetables, and pastries.

- **Robotics Research**: Commonly utilized in research and development settings for exploring new ways to interact with objects and environments.

- **Manufacturing**: Employed in assembly lines where delicate components need to be handled carefully, such as electronics and optical devices.

- **Healthcare**: Utilized in medical robotics for handling sensitive instruments and devices without causing damage.

3.15 Three-Fingered Grippers

Three-fingered grippers are robotic end-effectors designed with three movable fingers, allowing for more versatile and adaptive grasping of various objects. These grippers are commonly used in robotic applications that require intricate handling and manipulation of items with different shapes and sizes.

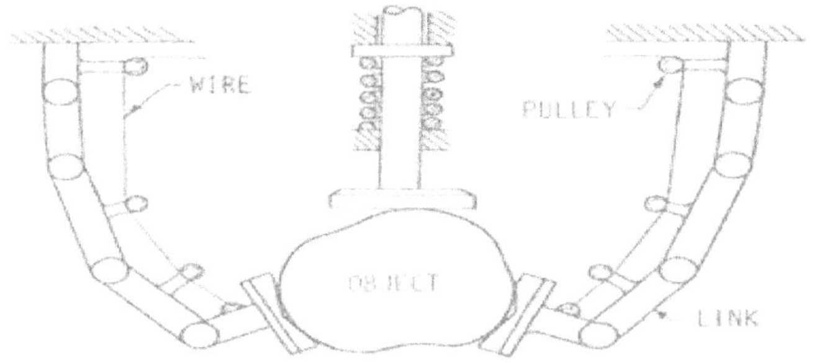

Fig 3.10: Three Fingered Grippers

Mechanism:

- **Finger Configuration**: Typically, three-fingered grippers consist of three opposing fingers that can move independently or in coordination. This configuration allows for a more secure and stable grip on irregularly shaped objects.

- **Types of Movements**:
  - **Beat Movement**: One type of clamping movement where the fingers move in a manner similar to a "beating" motion,

effectively grasping the object from multiple sides.

- o **Bite Movement**: In this movement, the fingers mimic a biting action, helping to encircle the object for a secure grip.
- o **Parallel Movement of the Jaw**: This involves moving the fingers in a parallel manner to grasp objects uniformly, ensuring a secure hold without tilting or dropping the object.

Advantages:

1. **Enhanced Grasping Capability**: The three-finger design allows for better adaptation to various object shapes, providing a more stable grip.

2. **Versatility**: Capable of handling a wider range of objects compared to two-fingered grippers, making them suitable for more complex tasks.

3. **Improved Load Distribution**: The distribution of forces across three points of contact reduces the risk of damaging delicate objects.

4. **Precision Manipulation**: They offer improved control and precision for tasks requiring intricate handling, such as assembly operations.

Limitations:

- **Complex Control**: Controlling three independent fingers can complicate the design and require more advanced algorithms for effective manipulation.

- **Increased Size and Weight**: Three-fingered grippers may be larger and heavier than two-fingered designs, potentially affecting the robot's overall efficiency.

- **Cost**: Generally, they may be more expensive to design and produce due to the complexity of their mechanisms.

Applications:

- **Robotic Surgery**: Utilized in surgical robots for precision manipulation of tools and instruments.

- **Manufacturing and Assembly**: Commonly used in industries where delicate components must be handled carefully, such as electronics and automotive assembly.

- **Material Handling**: Employed in logistics and warehousing for picking and placing items of varying shapes and sizes.

- **Research and Development**: Used in research labs to explore advanced gripping techniques and improve robotic manipulation.

Adhesive Grippers

- Adhesive grippers utilize an adhesive substance to grip objects, effectively holding items by adhering to one side only.
- **Mechanism**:
    - The adhesive material is applied to the gripper surface. When brought into contact with an object, it sticks to the surface due to adhesive properties.
    - To maintain grip effectiveness, the adhesive is often supplied as a continuous ribbon from a feeding mechanism attached to the robot wrist.
- **Limitations**:
    - Adhesive properties diminish after repeated use, reducing reliability.
    - Not suitable for items that need to be gripped on multiple sides or those with uneven surfaces.

3.16 Hooks and Scoops

- **Hooks**:
    - Used as end-effectors for handling containers and loading/unloading parts from overhead conveyors.

- o Require items to have a handle or some form of attachment point to grip effectively.

- **Scoops**:
  - o Designed for handling materials in liquid or powder form.
  - o One limitation is the difficulty in controlling the amount of material being scooped, leading to potential spillage.

3.17 Introduction to Manipulators

- Robotic manipulators are arm-like mechanisms designed to perform various tasks such as picking and placing objects, emulating human arm movements.

- **Structure**:
  - o Composed of sliding or jointed segments, manipulators have a fixed end and a free end to perform tasks.
  - o They consist of an arm (with joints and links) and a wrist (for tool manipulation).

- **Performance Factors**:
  - o Speed, payload weight, and precision are critical to the manipulator's functionality.
  - o Reach and workspace are determined by the manipulator's design and joint configuration.

3.18 Kinematics of a Robotic Manipulator

- **Components**:
  - Rigid links connected by joints that enable motion.
  - Two types of joints: linear joints (for non-rotational movement) and rotary joints (for rotational movement).
- **Arm and Body**:
  - Includes large links connected by three joints, allowing for the movement of objects within the workspace.
- **Wrist Functionality**:
  - Arranges objects/tools at the workspace using compact joints (two or three).

3.19 Manipulator Configuration:

1. **Cartesian Arm**: Utilizes prismatic joints for rectangular workspace movement.
2. **Cylindrical Arm**: Combines translation and rotation for movement in a cylindrical workspace.
3. **Polar/Spherical Arm**: Uses polar coordinates for end-effector positioning.
4. **Articulated/ Revolute Arm**: Offers complex movement through revolute joints in a thick-walled shell.

5. **SCARA (Selective Compliance Assembly Robot Arm)**: Designed for horizontal planar extension with two revolute joints.

3.20 Robot Dynamics

- Dynamics deals with how forces and moments affect the motion of robotic systems, contrasting with kinematics, which focuses solely on motion without regard to forces.

- **Equations of Motion**:
  - Describes the relationship between input joint torques and output motion of the robot.
  - Two main methods for obtaining these equations:
    - **Newton-Euler Formulation**: Uses Newton's laws to account for forces and moments, incorporating all interactions between links.
    - **Lagrangian Formulation**: Uses work and energy principles, simplifying the equations by eliminating constraints.

Basic Dynamic Equations:

- **Rigid Body Motion**: Decomposed into translational and rotational motion.

- **Newton's Equation of Motion**: Governs translational motion of the center of mass.

- **Euler's Equation of Motion**: Governs rotational motion about the center of mass.

Inverse Dynamics Problem:

- Focuses on determining the necessary input torques to achieve a desired motion of the robot's linkage.

- Efficient algorithms enable real-time dynamic computations.

Model Questions

Part A Questions

1. Differentiate joint space and world space

2. Write the advantages of magnetic grippers.

3. What are the common types of motion that a manipulator can make?

4. What do you know about end effectors with unilateral and bilateral gripping action?

5. How are the robots classified on the basis of manipulator geometry?

6. Give two applications where vacuum grippers are widely used in robots.

7. What is inverse kinematics?

Part B Questions

1. Compare joint space versus Cartesian space trajectory planning techniques also discuss briefly about the factors governing dynamic performance of a robot?

2. Explain (a) Manipulator path control

      (b) Manipulator dynamics

3. Discuss the different types of mechanisms with neat diagrams.

4. Describe the type of power sources used in the manipulation of grippers for robotics

Chapter 4

Kinematics and path planning

In robotics, understanding the movement and positioning of robotic arms is crucial for tasks ranging from industrial automation to medical surgeries. This chapter delves into the fundamental concepts of kinematics and path planning, focusing on Forward Kinematics, the Denavit-Hartenberg (DH) Representation, Inverse Kinematics, and the Geometric Approach. We will explore how these principles enable robots to move precisely in their operational environments

4.1 Robot Kinematics

Robot kinematics applies geometry to the study of the movement of multi-degree-of-freedom kinematic chains that form the structure of robotic systems. The emphasis on geometry means that the links of the robot are modeled as rigid bodies, and its joints are assumed to provide pure rotation or translation.

Robot kinematics studies the relationship between the dimensions and connectivity of kinematic chains and the position, velocity, and acceleration of each of the links in the robotic system. This is crucial for planning and controlling movement, as well as for computing actuator forces and torques. The relationship between mass and inertia properties, motion, and the associated forces and torques is also studied as part of robot dynamics.

Robot kinematics concepts relate to both open and closed kinematic chains. **Forward kinematics** is distinguished from **inverse kinematics**:

- **Forward Kinematics**: This refers to the computation of the position and orientation of the end effector based on given joint parameters (angles for revolute joints or distances for prismatic joints).
- **Inverse Kinematics**: This involves determining the necessary joint parameters to achieve a desired position and orientation of the end effector.

4.2 Serial Manipulators

Serial manipulators are the most common type of industrial robots. They are designed as a series of links connected by motor-actuated joints, extending from a base to an end effector. Often, they have an anthropomorphic arm structure described as having a "shoulder," an "elbow," and a "wrist."

Typically, serial robots have six joints, as at least six degrees of freedom are required to place a manipulated object in an arbitrary position and orientation within the robot's workspace.

A popular application for serial robots in today's industry is the pick-and-place assembly robot, commonly known as a SCARA (Selective Compliance Assembly Robot Arm) robot, which has four degrees of freedom.

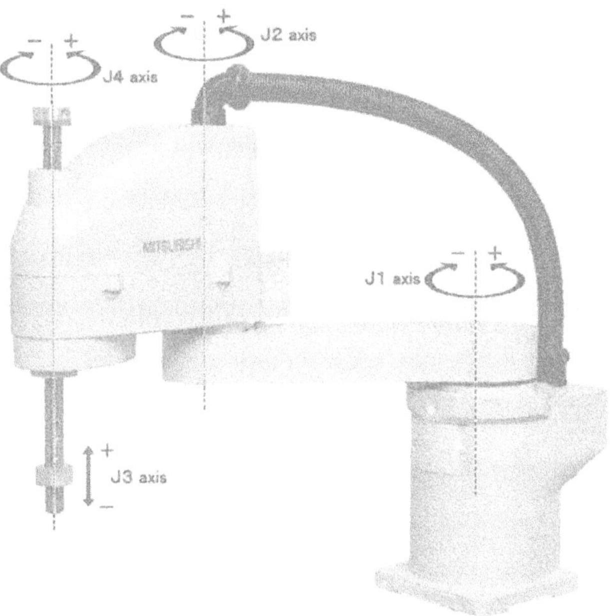

Fig 4.1: SCARA robot

4.3 SCARA Robot Axes

- **J1 Axis (Base Rotation)**:
  This axis allows the base of the robot to rotate,
  enabling the arm to turn around the vertical axis. It

178

is crucial for positioning the end effector within the horizontal workspace.

- **J2 Axis (Shoulder Joint)**:
The shoulder joint permits the first link of the arm to move in a vertical plane. This joint provides the ability to lift or lower the arm, contributing to the overall reach of the robot.

- **J3 Axis (Elbow Joint)**:
The elbow joint allows for additional vertical movement and is responsible for extending or retracting the arm. This joint plays a vital role in determining the reach and flexibility of the robot.

- **J4 Axis (Wrist Joint)**:
The wrist joint enables the end effector to rotate around its axis, allowing for precise orientation of tools or grippers. This joint is essential for tasks that require a specific angle or orientation of the end effector.

4.4 Structure of Serial Robots

In its most general form, a serial robot consists of a number of rigid links connected by joints. Simplicity considerations in manufacturing and control have led to the design of robots that utilize either revolute or prismatic joints, with orthogonal, parallel, and/or intersecting joint axes. The inverse kinematics of serial manipulators with six revolute joints, particularly those with three consecutive intersecting joints, can be solved in closed form, meaning that analytical solutions are possible. This capability has had a tremendous influence on the design of industrial robots.

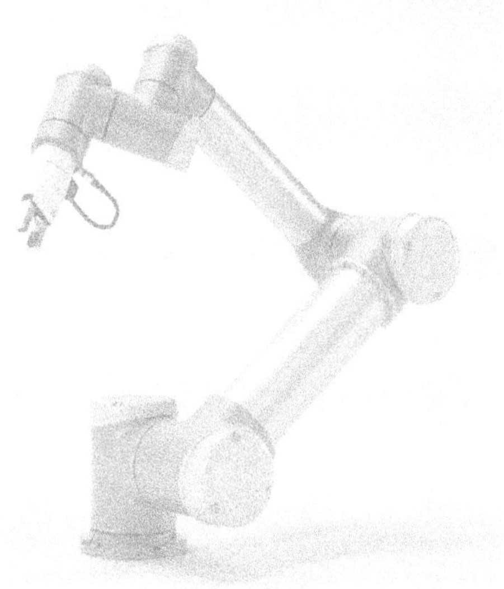

Fig.4.2: Serial manipulator with six DOF in a kinematic chain

4.5 Advantages of Serial Manipulators:

- **Large Workspace**: Serial manipulators offer a large workspace relative to the size of the robot and the floor space it occupies, allowing for a wide range of motion and operational versatility.

Disadvantages of Serial Manipulators:

- **Low Stiffness**: The open kinematic structure leads to low stiffness, making the robot less stable during operations.

- **Error Accumulation**: Errors in positioning can accumulate and amplify from link to link, reducing overall accuracy.

- **Weight of Actuators**: Serial robots must carry and move the large weight of most actuators, which can limit their efficiency and increase energy consumption.

- **Low Effective Load Capacity**: They typically have a relatively low effective load capacity, which may restrict their application in heavy-duty tasks.

4.6 Parallel Manipulator

A parallel manipulator is a mechanical system that uses several computer-controlled serial chains to support a single platform, or end-effector. One of the best-known parallel manipulators is the **Stewart platform** (also called the **Gough-Stewart platform**), which consists of six linear actuators that support a movable base, often used in devices like flight simulators. This platform is named in recognition of the engineers who first designed and utilized it.

Also referred to as **parallel robots** or **generalized Stewart platforms**, these systems are articulated robots that use similar mechanisms for the movement of either the robot on its base or one or more manipulator arms. The term "parallel" here refers to the fact that the end-effector (or "hand") of the manipulator is connected to its base by multiple (usually three or six) separate and independent linkages working simultaneously.

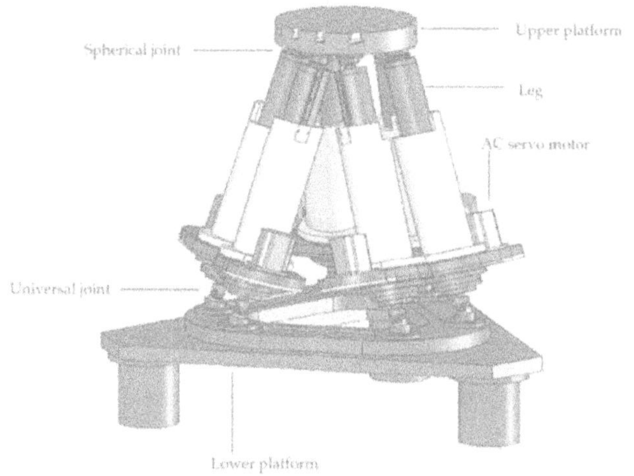

Fig:4.3: Abstract render of a Hexapod platform
(Stewart Platform)

Unlike serial manipulators, where joints and links are connected in a series, parallel manipulators have linkages that work in **parallel**. This means the position of each linkage endpoint is independent of the others, allowing for more stable and precise movements. The use of "parallel" in this context refers to the computer science concept, meaning that the linkages act together, not that they are geometrically aligned in parallel lines.

Forward Kinematics:

- Forward kinematics is used to determine the position and orientation of the robot's end-effector (or "hand") when all the joint variables (such as angles for revolute joints or distances for prismatic joints) are known.

- **Purpose**: It helps in calculating the exact location of the end-effector based on the given positions of each joint in the robot.

Inverse Kinematics:

- Inverse kinematics is used to calculate the required joint variables that will position the robot's end-effector at a desired location and orientation.

- **Purpose**: It helps in determining what each joint's parameters should be if we want the end-effector to reach a specific point in space.

4.7 Robots as Mechanisms

Robots can be viewed as complex mechanisms composed of interconnected mechanical components, such as links and joints, which enable controlled motion. In this context, a robot is essentially a machine designed to execute tasks with precision, flexibility, and autonomy, using mechanical and electronic systems.

Key Aspects of Robots as Mechanisms:

1. **Links and Joints**:

   Robots are constructed with rigid bodies called **links** connected by **joints** (either revolute or prismatic) that allow relative movement. These joints act as points of motion, similar to hinges or sliders in mechanical systems.

2. **Degrees of Freedom (DOF)**:

   The degrees of freedom refer to the number of independent movements a robot can make. Each joint adds a degree of freedom, determining the robot's ability to maneuver within its workspace. Robots generally require at least six DOF to position and orient an end-effector in three-dimensional space.

3. **Kinematic Chains**:

A robot's structure can be described as a **kinematic chain**, which is a sequence of links and joints. **Serial manipulators** have open chains, where each link is connected in sequence from the base to the end-effector. **Parallel manipulators** use multiple closed chains working simultaneously to control the end-effector.

4. **Actuators**:

Actuators are devices that move the joints, providing motion to the robot. These can be electric motors, hydraulic systems, or pneumatic cylinders. The combination of actuators and joints defines how the robot moves and interacts with its environment.

5. **End-Effector**:

The **end-effector** is the tool attached to the robot's last link, and it performs the desired task, such as gripping, welding, or painting. It is the functional component that interacts with the external world.

6. **Control Systems**:

Robots operate based on control systems that dictate the movement of joints, the path of motion, and the specific tasks to be carried out. These systems use feedback from sensors to ensure precision and adjust motions as needed.

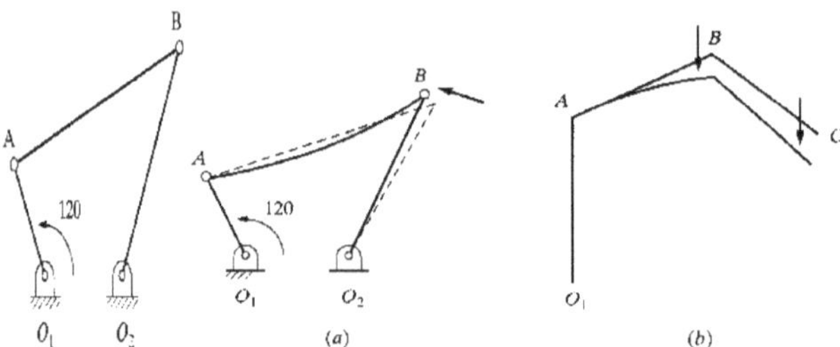

Fig 4.4: a one – degree – of - freedom closed-loop(a) Closed-loop versus (b) open-loop mechanism Four-barmechanism

The distinction between **closed-loop** and **open-loop** mechanisms is fundamental in understanding mechanical systems and robotic kinematics, especially when discussing a **four-bar mechanism**.

1. Closed-Loop Mechanism (One-Degree-of-Freedom Example):

- A **closed-loop mechanism** is a mechanical system where all the components form a loop, with one or more kinematic chains closing on themselves. The movement of each link is constrained by the others, and the motion is interdependent.

- **Degrees of Freedom**: A **one-degree-of-freedom (1-DOF) closed-loop mechanism** means that the entire system's motion can be controlled by a single input (such as a motor or actuator). In this type of mechanism, once the input is provided, all the other links move in a constrained, predictable pattern.

Example: Four-Bar Mechanism

A common example of a one-degree-of-freedom closed-loop system is the **four-bar mechanism**.

Structure of a Four-Bar Mechanism:

- **Links**: It consists of four rigid links: the input link (driven by an actuator), the coupler link, the output link, and the ground link (which is fixed).

- **Joints**: These links are connected by revolute joints, forming a loop.

  In this mechanism:

- The movement of one link (the input) drives the motion of the others.

- The output link follows a predetermined path, providing controlled motion, often used in applications like levers or robotic arms.

2. Open-Loop Mechanism:

- In an **open-loop mechanism**, the links are connected in sequence without forming a loop. The motion of each link is typically independent, and there's no feedback or constraint that links the movement of one part to another.

- **Degrees of Freedom**: Open-loop mechanisms typically have multiple degrees of freedom, meaning multiple actuators or motors are needed to control each movement individually.

Comparison:

Aspect	Closed-Loop Mechanism (e.g., Four-Bar Mechanism)	Open-Loop Mechanism
Motion	Constrained, interdependent motion of all links	Independent movement of each link
Degrees of Freedom	Typically fewer (e.g., 1 DOF)	Can have multiple DOF
Control	Controlled by a single actuator	Requires multiple actuators
Stability	Higher stability due to interconnected structure	Less constrained, more flexibility
Feedback	Relies on constraints for movement	Usually no feedback between links

(a) Closed-Loop vs (b) Open-Loop Mechanism: In **closed-loop** systems, like the four-bar mechanism, all movements are interdependent, forming a constrained motion. In contrast, **open-loop** mechanisms consist of serial chains where each joint can move independently, with no inherent feedback between joints.

4.8 Matrix Representation:

Representation of a Point in Space

In robotics and kinematics, matrix representation is widely used to represent points, vectors, and transformations in space. A **point P** in space is typically described using coordinates relative to a reference frame.

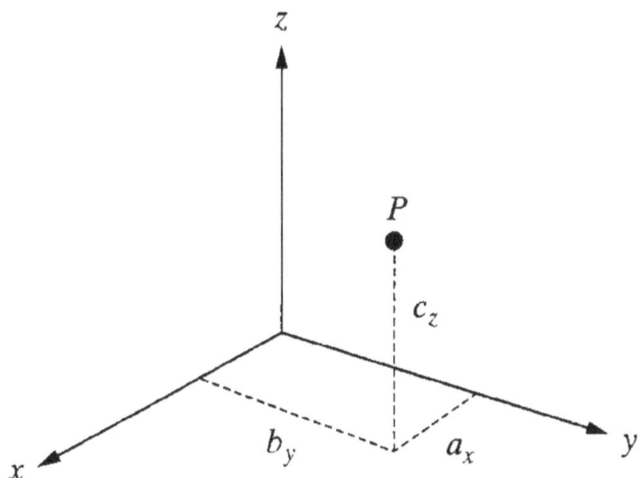

Fig.4.5: Representation of a point in space

Here's how it works:

4.8.1. Representation of a Point in 3D Space:

A point P in three-dimensional space is described by three coordinates: x, y, and z, which define its position relative to a reference frame (usually called the world frame or base frame).

Matrix Form:

The position of the point P can be represented as a column vector (3x1 matrix):

$P=[x\ y\ z]$

Here:

- x is the coordinate of P along the **x-axis**,
- y is the coordinate of P along the **y-axis**,
- z is the coordinate of P along the **z-axis**.

This matrix form allows for straightforward manipulation of the point's position using transformations like rotation and translation.

4.8.2. Homogeneous Coordinates:

To simplify the representation of transformations (e.g., rotation and translation), a 3D point can be represented in **homogeneous coordinates**, where an extra dimension is added to facilitate matrix multiplication.

The homogeneous representation of point P is given by:

Ph=[x y z 1]

The last element, 1, is the homogeneous coordinate, which helps in performing affine transformations, including translations.

4.8.3. Reference Frame:

The point P is defined relative to a **reference frame** (a coordinate system with origin and axes). The reference frame may be static (such as the world frame) or dynamic (attached to a moving object, like a robot's link).

- The transformation between different reference frames, such as from a local frame to the world frame, is done through **transformation matrices** (composed of both rotation and translation).

Example of Representation in 3D:

If point P is located at coordinates (3, 4, 5) in a given reference frame, its matrix representation is:

P=[3 4 5]

In homogeneous coordinates:

P_s=[3 4 5 1]

4. Transformation of a Point in Space:

When applying transformations like rotations or translations to point P, you multiply it by transformation matrices. For example:

- **Rotation Matrix**: Changes the orientation of the point in space.

- **Translation Matrix**: Shifts the point by a certain distance along one or more axes.

For example, if we apply a translation by tx,ty,tz to point P_{hP}, we use the translation matrix:

$$T = \begin{bmatrix} 1 & 0 & 0 & t_x \\ 0 & 1 & 0 & t_y \\ 0 & 0 & 1 & t_z \\ 0 & 0 & 0 & 1 \end{bmatrix}$$

Multiplying this matrix with P_h results in the new position of the point after translation.

4.9 Representation of a Vector in Space

A vector in space can be represented by specifying the coordinates of its **tail** (starting point) and its **head** (end point). A vector describes a quantity with both magnitude and direction, and it can be used to represent motion, force, or position changes in robotics and other mechanical systems.

4.9.1. Basic Representation of a Vector:

A vector $\vec{P}$ in three-dimensional space is typically represented as:

$$\vec{P} = \begin{bmatrix} P_x \\ P_y \\ P_z \end{bmatrix}$$

where:

- Px,Py,PzP represent the components of the vector along the **x**, **y**, and **z** axes, respectively.

4.9.2. Coordinates of the Tail and Head:

A vector in space can be visualized by specifying two points:

- **Tail (starting point)**: $P_{tail}(x1,y1,z1)$

- **Head (end point)**: $P_{head}(x2,y2,z2)$

The vector $\vec{P}$ is the difference between the coordinates of the head and the tail:

$$\vec{P} = \begin{bmatrix} x_2 - x_1 \\ y_2 - y_1 \\ z_2 - z_1 \end{bmatrix}$$

Here, x2−x1, y2−y1, and z2−z1 represent the changes along the respective axes, defining the direction and magnitude of the vector.

4.9.3. Magnitude of the Vector:

The magnitude (or length) of the vector P⃗is given by the Euclidean distance between the tail and head:

$$|\vec{P}| = \sqrt{(x_2 - x_1)^2 + (y_2 - y_1)^2 + (z_2 - z_1)^2}$$

This magnitude represents the distance between the two points in space.

4.9.4. Direction of the Vector:

The direction of the vector P⃗is given by the ratios of its components to its magnitude:

$$\hat{P} = \frac{\vec{P}}{|\vec{P}|} = \begin{bmatrix} \dfrac{x_2 - x_1}{|\vec{P}|} \\[2mm] \dfrac{y_2 - y_1}{|\vec{P}|} \\[2mm] \dfrac{z_2 - z_1}{|\vec{P}|} \end{bmatrix}$$

This unit vector P^ describes the direction of the vector without considering its magnitude.

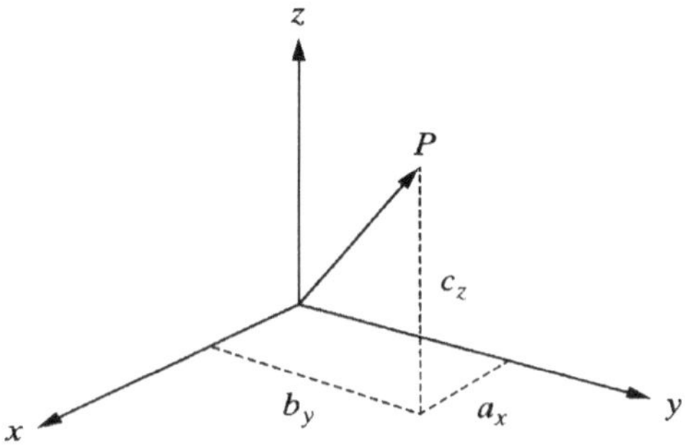

Fig.4.6: Representation of a vector in space

Model Questions

Part A

1. What is robot kinematics, and why is it important in robotics?

2. Define serial manipulators and give an example.

3. What does SCARA stand for in robotics?

4. Name the axes used by SCARA robots and describe one characteristic of SCARA robots.

5. Briefly explain the structure of a serial robot.

6. List two advantages of using serial manipulators in robotics.

7. What is a parallel manipulator, and how is it different from a serial manipulator?

8. Why are robots often described as mechanisms in kinematics?

9. What is the purpose of matrix representation in robot kinematics?

10. How does matrix representation help in understanding robot motion?

11. Explain what a vector in space represents in the context of robot kinematics.

12. Describe one application where a serial manipulator would be beneficial.

13. What is the main functional difference between serial and parallel manipulators?

14. In what ways does a SCARA robot differ from a typical Cartesian robot?

15. How does the representation of vectors in space contribute to robot path planning?

Chapter 5

Programming Languages and Applications

Robotics is an interdisciplinary field that combines engineering, computer science, and technology to create machines capable of performing tasks autonomously or semi-autonomously. The rapid evolution of robotics has led to significant advancements in programming languages tailored to the unique needs of robotic applications. This chapter explores recent trends in programming languages used in robotics, their applications, and the impact these languages have on the field.

5.1. The Role of Programming Languages in Robotics

Programming languages are essential in robotics for controlling hardware, processing data from sensors, implementing algorithms for perception and navigation, and facilitating human-robot interaction. The choice of programming language can greatly influence the performance, efficiency, and ease of development of robotic systems.

5.1.1. Communication with Hardware

Robots consist of various hardware components, including sensors, actuators, and processors. Programming languages act as an interface between these components and the algorithms that control them.

- **Low-Level Programming**: Languages like C and C++ allow developers to write low-level code that directly interacts with hardware, providing fine control over timing, resource management, and performance.

- **Hardware Abstraction**: High-level languages, such as Python, provide libraries that abstract the complexities of hardware communication. This abstraction allows developers to focus on algorithm development rather than the intricacies of hardware control.

5.1.2. Algorithm Implementation

At the core of robotics lies the need for algorithms that enable perception, decision-making, and movement. Programming languages facilitate the implementation of these algorithms through structured code and robust libraries.

- **Sensor Processing**: Languages like Python and C++ are widely used to process data from sensors (e.g., cameras, LiDAR, IMUs) to interpret the robot's environment. For instance, computer vision algorithms can be implemented to enable visual perception in robots.

- **Path Planning and Navigation**: Algorithms for path planning, such as A* and Dijkstra's algorithm, can be implemented in various programming languages to help robots navigate through complex environments.

5.13. Simulation and Testing

Before deploying robots in real-world scenarios, extensive testing and simulation are crucial. Programming languages play a vital role in creating virtual environments for testing and validating robotic systems.

- **Simulation Frameworks**: Tools like Gazebo and Webots are often programmed using languages like C++ and Python, allowing developers to simulate robot behavior in a controlled environment.

- **Algorithm Verification**: By running simulations, developers can verify the performance of algorithms under different conditions, identifying potential issues before physical deployment.

5.14. Rapid Prototyping and Development

The ability to quickly develop and iterate on robotic systems is essential, especially in research and development contexts. Programming languages significantly impact the speed and efficiency of this process.

- **High-Level Languages**: Languages such as Python and MATLAB are favored for rapid prototyping due to their readability and the availability of extensive libraries for tasks like data analysis, machine learning, and robotics (e.g., ROS).

- **Modular Development**: Programming languages enable modular design, where different components of a robotic system can be developed and tested independently, facilitating easier integration and faster development cycles.

5.1.5. Interoperability and Collaboration

Robotics is inherently interdisciplinary, often requiring collaboration between engineers, computer scientists, and domain experts. Programming languages play a crucial role in fostering interoperability and facilitating collaboration.

- **Standardized Protocols**: Languages that adhere to standardized communication protocols (e.g., ROS, MQTT) allow different systems and components to work together seamlessly, regardless of the underlying programming language used.

- **Open Source Libraries**: The availability of open-source libraries and frameworks in languages like Python and C++ encourages collaboration among researchers and developers, fostering innovation in the field.

5.1.6. Human-Robot Interaction

As robots increasingly operate in environments shared with humans, programming languages are essential for developing interfaces that facilitate interaction.

- **User Interfaces**: Programming languages like Java and Python are used to create graphical user interfaces (GUIs) for controlling and monitoring robotic systems, allowing users to interact with robots intuitively.

- **Natural Language Processing**: With the rise of conversational interfaces, languages that support natural language processing (e.g., Python with libraries like NLTK) enable robots to understand and respond to human commands.

5.1.7. Future Directions

The role of programming languages in robotics will continue to evolve, influenced by emerging technologies and changing industry demands. Some potential future directions include:

- **Increased Focus on Safety and Security**: As robots become more integrated into daily life, programming languages that prioritize safety and security (e.g., Rust) will gain prominence.

- **Integration of AI and Machine Learning**: Programming languages that facilitate the integration of AI and machine learning algorithms will be crucial for developing more intelligent and adaptable robotic systems.

- **Edge Computing**: As robotics moves towards edge computing, languages that support lightweight applications and efficient processing will be critical for real-time decision-making in robotics.

Programming languages are indispensable in the field of robotics, shaping how robots are designed, built, and operated. They enable communication with hardware, support algorithm implementation, facilitate simulation and testing, and foster collaboration among diverse teams. As the field of robotics continues to advance, the role of programming languages will remain central to driving innovation and improving robotic capabilities, making it a vital area of study for engineers and developers alike.

5.2. Recent Trends in Programming Languages for Robotics

The field of robotics has advanced rapidly, driven by the need for intelligent systems that can interact autonomously and seamlessly with real-world environments. Programming languages for robotics have evolved to meet the increasing demands of complex algorithms, real-time processing, and efficient control mechanisms. The recent trends in this domain reflect a shift towards languages and frameworks that prioritize flexibility, ease of integration, and support for AI-driven tasks.

Languages such as Python, ROS (Robot Operating System), and C++ dominate the landscape due to their robust libraries, community support, and performance capabilities suited to robotics applications. Python, with its simplicity and extensive machine learning libraries, has become popular for prototyping and integrating AI features, while C++ is often used for time-critical tasks due to its performance advantages. ROS, an open-source framework, has established itself as a cornerstone in robotics programming, providing standardized tools and packages that enable developers to focus on application-specific tasks without reinventing the wheel. Additionally, new languages like Julia and Rust are gaining traction in robotics, with Julia offering high-performance numerical computing and Rust providing memory-safe programming, both important in robotics applications.

These trends highlight an emphasis on hybrid systems where multiple languages are often used in tandem, allowing for optimized performance and rapid development cycles. As robotic applications continue to grow, the choice of programming languages and frameworks will play a crucial role in determining how effectively robots can adapt to and operate in dynamic environments.

5.2.1 Python: The Language of Choice for Rapid Prototyping

- Python's simplicity and extensive libraries make it a popular choice in robotics, especially for rapid prototyping and research.
- **Applications**:
  - **Robot Operating System (ROS)**: Python is widely used in ROS, a flexible framework

for writing robot software. It allows developers to build modular systems where different components communicate seamlessly.

- o **Machine Learning and AI**: With libraries like TensorFlow and PyTorch, Python is increasingly used for implementing machine learning algorithms in robotics. This enables robots to learn from data and improve their performance over time.

5.2.2 C++: The Backbone of Performance-Critical Robotics

- C++ is known for its performance and control over system resources, making it ideal for low-level programming in robotics.

- **Applications**:
  - o **Real-Time Systems**: Many robotic applications, such as autonomous vehicles and industrial robots, require real-time processing. C++ provides the performance necessary for these applications.

  - o **Embedded Systems**: C++ is extensively used in programming microcontrollers and embedded systems, which are integral to the hardware of robots.

5.2.3 Java: Versatility and Cross-Platform Development

- Java's platform independence and strong object-oriented features make it suitable for large-scale robotic systems.

- **Applications**:
  - **Mobile Robotics**: Java is used in mobile robotics applications, especially in developing applications for Android devices, enabling mobile robots to process data and communicate.
  - **Simulation and Control**: Java-based frameworks are used for simulating robotic environments and controlling robots in various applications, from logistics to healthcare.

5.2.4 ROS (Robot Operating System) and Its Influence

- While not a programming language per se, ROS is a significant framework that influences programming practices in robotics.

- **Applications**:
  - **Modular Software Development**: ROS enables developers to create reusable code

modules, fostering collaboration and reducing development time.

- o **Interoperability**: By providing tools and libraries for various programming languages (like Python and C++), ROS enhances interoperability among robotic systems, allowing them to work together seamlessly.

5.2.5. MATLAB: Simulation and Algorithm Development

- MATLAB is widely used in academia and industry for modeling, simulation, and algorithm development in robotics.
- **Applications**:
  - o **Simulation Environments**: MATLAB's Simulink provides a platform for simulating robotic systems before deployment, allowing engineers to test and optimize algorithms safely.
  - o **Control System Design**: MATLAB is used to design and analyze control systems for robots, ensuring they perform tasks accurately and efficiently.

5.2.6 Swift and Rust: Emerging Languages in Robotics

- Swift and Rust are gaining traction in specific robotics applications due to their modern features and safety.

- **Applications**:
  - **Swift for iOS Robotics Apps**: Swift is used to develop applications for controlling robots via mobile devices, leveraging the growing trend of smartphone integration in robotics.

  - **Rust for Safety-Critical Systems**: Rust's emphasis on memory safety and performance makes it suitable for robotics applications where reliability is paramount, such as in autonomous vehicles.

5.3. Applications of Programming Languages in Robotics

In robotics, the choice of programming language significantly influences a robot's functionality, performance, and ability to integrate advanced features. Each programming language brings unique strengths, from real-time processing to AI integration, shaping how robots perceive, analyze, and interact with their surroundings.

Selecting an appropriate language is essential for developing efficient, flexible, and robust robotic systems capable of executing complex tasks across various industries.

Here are some prominent applications of programming languages in robotics:

Motion Control and Path Planning

Languages like C++ and Python are widely used in developing motion control algorithms, which ensure precise movements and accurate path planning. C++ is often preferred for its speed and efficiency in handling the low-level computations required for real-time control.

Computer Vision and Image Processing

Python, with libraries such as OpenCV and TensorFlow, is commonly applied to enable robots to interpret visual data, detect objects, and navigate based on visual cues. This is crucial for applications in automated manufacturing, autonomous vehicles, and medical robotics.

Artificial Intelligence and Machine Learning

Python, due to its extensive ML and AI libraries (e.g., TensorFlow, PyTorch), is frequently chosen for integrating intelligent decision-making into robots, allowing them to recognize patterns, perform natural language processing, and learn from data.

Sensor Integration and Data Fusion

The Robot Operating System (ROS) supports Python and C++ and is integral in fusing data from multiple sensors, like LIDAR, GPS, and cameras. This allows robots to achieve situational awareness, critical for autonomous navigation and collision avoidance.

Embedded and Real-Time Systems

C and C++ are ideal for embedded programming and real-time applications due to their efficiency and control over hardware resources, making them essential in building fast, responsive robotic systems with strict timing requirements.

Simulation and Testing

Robotics developers use languages like Python with ROS or specialized simulation tools (Gazebo, Webots) for virtual testing, allowing for experimentation in a simulated environment before deploying robots in real-world scenarios.

These applications illustrate the diverse ways in which programming languages contribute to the functionality and innovation of robotic systems across industries, underscoring the importance of language choice in achieving specialized robotic capabilities. Here are some prominent applications:

5.3.1. Industrial Robotics

- **Programming Languages**: C++, Python
- **Applications**: Used for programming robotic arms in manufacturing processes, including assembly, welding, and painting. Languages enable real-time processing and integration with other systems.

5.3.2. Autonomous Vehicles

- **Programming Languages**: C++, Python, MATLAB
- **Applications**: Languages are used for navigation algorithms, sensor fusion, and machine learning models that enable vehicles to understand their environment and make decisions.

5.3.3. Service Robotics

- **Programming Languages**: Python, Java, Swift
- **Applications**: In service robotics, such as delivery robots or cleaning robots, programming languages

are used for path planning, obstacle detection, and user interface development.

5.3.4. Robotic Simulation

- **Programming Languages**: Python, C++, MATLAB
- **Applications**: Simulation tools allow engineers to test algorithms and models in virtual environments, reducing costs and risks associated with real-world testing.

5.4. Future Directions and Conclusion

As robotics continues to evolve, the programming languages used will also adapt to meet new challenges and demands. Future trends may include:

- **Increased Use of AI and Machine Learning**: Languages that facilitate the integration of AI and ML capabilities will become increasingly important.
- **Greater Emphasis on Safety and Security**: As robots operate in more complex environments, programming languages that prioritize safety and reliability, like Rust, will gain traction.
- **Interdisciplinary Collaboration**: The convergence of robotics with other fields, such as biotechnology

and materials science, will necessitate languages that support collaboration across disciplines.

Model Questions (5 Marks Each)

Part A

1. What are the benefits of using high-level programming languages in robotics? Can you give some examples of where these languages are especially useful?

2. What is the Robot Operating System (ROS) and why is it important in robotics? How does it help programmers use different languages?

3. What are domain-specific languages (DSLs) in robotics? What are their advantages, and can you name some common DSLs used in this field?

4. How does the use of AI and machine learning affect the programming languages chosen for robotics? What does this mean for what robots can do?

5. Why is safety and security important in the programming languages used for robots? How do languages like Rust help keep robots safe in important situations?